WORK STRONGER

WORK STRONGER

HABITS FOR MORE ENERGY, LESS STRESS, AND HIGHER PERFORMANCE AT WORK

PETE LEIBMAN

Skyhorse Publishing

Skyhorse Publishing books may be purchased in bulk at special discounts for sales promotion, corporate gifts, fund-raising, or educational purposes. Special editions can also be created to specifications. For details, contact the Special Sales Department, Skyhorse Publishing, 307 West 36th Street, 11th Floor, New York, NY 10018 or info@skyhorsepublishing.com.

Skyhorse® and Skyhorse Publishing® are registered trademarks of Skyhorse Publishing, Inc.®, a Delaware corporation.

Visit our website at www.skyhorsepublishing.com.

10 9 8 7 6 5 4 3 2 1

Library of Congress Cataloging-in-Publication Data is available on file.

Cover design by Rain Saukas

Print ISBN: 978-1-5107-3162-2
Ebook ISBN: 978-1-5107-3166-0

Printed in the United States of America

CONTENTS

INTRODUCTION

A small daily task, if it be really daily, will beat the labours of a spasmodic Hercules.
—Anthony Trollope, a nineteenth-century English novelist

An excerpt from a conversation that I had with my friend Tony (eighty-two days before the manuscript for *Work Stronger* was due):

Tony: What are your plans for the summer?

Pete: A few weekend trips, but I'm focused on finishing a book that I'm writing called *Work Stronger*.

Tony: Oh, really? What's the book about?

Pete: It's a book about the connection between healthier, stronger habits and higher performance at work.

Tony: I read an article recently that said that Warren Buffett drinks five cans of Coca-Cola a day. His net worth is supposedly over seventy-five billion dollars. What would your book have to say about that?

Pete: Imagine what Buffett might be worth if he didn't drink so much soda.

It's possible to reach the top of your field if you drink five sodas a day, if you have a sedentary lifestyle, or if you sleep fewer than six hours a night. It's also possible to complete a 26.2-mile marathon by doing cartwheels, by jogging backwards, or by crawling on your hands and knees. However, just because something is possible, that doesn't mean it's a smart strategy.

"The Success Delusion" is a concept from Dr. Marshall Goldsmith, a *New York Times* #1 best-selling author who has also been recognized as the world's #1 executive coach.[1] As Dr. Goldsmith writes in *What Got You Here Won't Get You There: How Successful People Become Even More Successful,* "One of the greatest mistakes successful people make is the assumption, 'I behave this way, and I achieve results. Therefore, I must be achieving results because I behave this way.'"[2]

When you are successful, it can be tempting to think that all of your behavior has contributed to your success. However, no one's behavior is perfect. There are always ways that you hold yourself back, no matter how much you have accomplished.

The fact that you are currently reading a book on high performance suggests that you are already a pretty successful person. *Work Stronger* will assist you in taking your performance to an even higher level by helping you discover and change behaviors that you are successful *in spite of* doing or not doing.

WHY YOU SHOULD READ THIS BOOK

You can be so much stronger than you realize. However, today's world can easily make you weaker—physically, mentally, and psychologically. This is due to the following three key reasons.

Today's Environment Encourages Unhealthy, Sedentary Behavior.

For most of human history, natural foods were your only option, and you had to be active to get food and to survive. Today's world could not be more different. Our ancestors did not have easy, ubiquitous access to sugary beverages, doughy treats, and heavily processed "foods" that provide empty calories and fleeting, uneven energy. Our ancestors also did not have access to computers, televisions, and other forms of technology that allow us to work or be entertained for hours without moving.

It is well known that poor nutrition and a sedentary lifestyle can make you overweight. It is also well known that being overweight increases your chances of developing virtually every chronic disease or condition, including cancer, diabetes, stroke, heart disease, and depression.

These are not the only consequences, though. An unhealthy lifestyle also reduces your intellectual horsepower and causes your brain to age faster. A 2016 study published in *Neurobiology of Aging* showed that brainpower declines faster for overweight people than for people who are leaner. Overweight subjects in the study had brains that resembled leaner subjects who were ten years older.[3]

Today's Environment Discourages Focus.

Laptops, smartphones, and other forms of technology clearly make our lives better in many ways. However, they also discourage us from concentrating on one task at a time. For example, a 2013 study commissioned by Nokia found that the average person checks his or her cell phone 150 times a day.[4] That's once every six to seven minutes, on average, during waking hours.

Despite what many people think, multitasking makes you less productive, not more productive. In fact, multitasking reduces your performance on virtually every kind of task...including your ability to multitask. Dr. Clifford Nass (a deceased Stanford University sociologist) studied this topic before he passed away. As he said during an interview in 2013, "People who multitask all the time can't filter out irrelevancy. They can't manage a working memory. They're chronically distracted. They initiate much larger parts of their brain that are irrelevant to the task at hand...they're even terrible at multitasking. When we ask them to multitask, they're actually worse at it."[5]

Today's Environment Discourages Renewal.

We are led to believe the myth that working longer automatically leads to better output. Many employers and leaders reinforce this fallacy. In most companies, you are more likely to be praised for finishing late than for finishing early.

When you work longer hours, something needs to give. Many people choose to cut back on sleep and other forms of personal renewal. This unfortunately makes matters even worse. Sleep deprivation reduces brainpower in the short term, and is also linked to obesity and virtually every other chronic disease or condition.[6]

The pressure in today's workplace can be tremendous at any level, whether you are a CEO, a middle manager, or an entry-level employee. If you want to thrive now, and as you advance throughout your career, you need to *work stronger*, not longer. **Stronger hours (not longer hours) are the key to feeling and performing your best over the long term.**

Stronger Habits = Stronger Hours

Research by Duke University has demonstrated that at least 40 percent of our daily actions are habitual.[7] In *Work Stronger*, you will learn how to take control of your behavior and form stronger habits in four key areas (nutrition, exercise, focus, and renewal) that are highly correlated with better health, well-being, and performance over the long term. Stronger habits will make you healthier, more energetic, more resilient, more confident, and more productive—so that you can achieve more in less time and with less stress.

THE STORY BEHIND THIS BOOK

As a fifteen-year-old student, I was 5'10" and had size thirteen sneakers, while only weighing 119 pounds. I looked like a "human L." There's no way that either of us would have predicted then that I would eventually write a book with the word "stronger" in the title.

After transforming my body at the end of high school through strength training and better eating habits, I became obsessed with seeing what else could be improved. Since then, I've spent more than fifteen years studying behavior change, psychology, and high performance. I majored in psychology at Johns Hopkins University (JHU), and I also worked as a fitness trainer for JHU while I was a student there. My first personal training client was the wife of JHU's president at that time. No pressure there, huh?

Since college, I've coached people privately and taught Sports Conditioning classes for hundreds of people who live in the Washington, D.C. area. I've also competed in many endurance obstacle races, including the Obstacle Course Racing (OCR) World Championships, an international event with athletes from more than forty countries.

However, most of my career has been spent inside of an office, perhaps like you. For the five years before this book was published,

I worked as an executive recruiter at Heidrick & Struggles, a leadership advisory firm that serves the majority of the Fortune 500. In this role, my main responsibility was to identify, interview, and assess executives for leadership roles.

Over the years, many people have asked me how to feel better and perform better. While I certainly don't have all the answers, this book will provide you with practical, step-by-step recommendations that are based on personal experience, interviews with high performers, and analysis of the latest scientific research. My mission in writing *Work Stronger* is to help you become the strongest, healthiest, and highest-performing person that you can be. Nothing brings me more joy than seeing other people overcome challenges and achieve their dreams.

My role as an author and coach is to expect and *demand* even more from you than you are currently expecting and demanding from yourself. If anything in this book comes off too strong, please consider my intention: to help you flourish. You cannot succeed beyond your wildest imagination without someone encouraging you and challenging you to be your best.

STRONGER HABITS (NOT GIMMICKS OR GENETICS)

Advertisements can mislead us and suggest that there are shortcuts to success. Billions of dollars are spent every year promoting products and services that promise you can look, feel, and perform better with little or no effort.

Life would be much easier if we could become our best over a weekend. Unfortunately, we cannot summon change in our lives as quickly as we can summon our next Uber. Significant changes occur slowly and with effort.

When you see people who are thriving (physically or in any other area of life), it is easy to assume they were born with better DNA. Your genetics can absolutely put you at a disadvantage or at an advantage. However, your genetics only determine where you start. Your *habits* determine where you finish. Isolated behaviors might not seem like a big deal. However, they add up quickly.

Consider the impact of one seemingly small bad habit. If you drink one sixteen-ounce sweetened iced tea today, that's only 150 calories and thirty-seven grams of sugar. That by itself is not a big deal. How-ever, that becomes a big deal when you do it every day, which would result in you consuming over 54,000 calories and over fifteen pounds of sugar over the next year. That's the same amount of sugar found in over 15,000 Skittles.[8] And that's one "small" bad habit!

The good news is that positive habits obviously add up as well. Consider the impact of one seemingly small good habit. If you eat one serving of spinach today, that's only three ounces of spinach. That by itself is not a big deal. However, that becomes a big deal—in a good way—when you do it every day, which would result in you consum-ing over sixty-eight pounds of one of the world's most nutrient-dense foods over the next year. And that's one "small" good habit.

You can achieve exceptional results in any area of your life by making changes that are simple and that might seem small. Stronger habits (not gimmicks or genetics) are the key to achieving and main-taining higher performance over the long term.

Part 1: The P.O.W.E.R. Pyramid

You don't need more willpower. As this book will demonstrate, peo-ple who are thriving are not "willing" themselves to greatness. They are forming stronger habits by thinking differently and by engineer-ing their lives in a very methodical way. They are tapping into a much stronger kind of P.O.W.E.R. that we will cover in detail in the first part of this book. Chapters 1–5 discuss *why* and *how* to form stronger habits. You will learn about a behavior change framework that I refer to as *The P.O.W.E.R. Pyramid.*

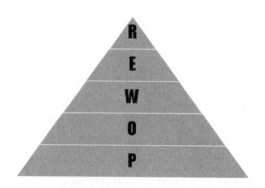

The P.O.W.E.R. Pyramid

Part 2: The Stronger Cycle

In the second part of this book, we will discuss a high-performance framework that I refer to as *The Stronger Cycle*. You will learn *what* to change in four key areas: nutrition, exercise, focus, and renewal. These areas have a significant impact on how you feel and perform. While everyone has unique goals and challenges, you will learn specific behaviors that yield incredible results. You will also learn how to personalize, adopt, and scale these habits for your lifestyle, both now and as you become even stronger.

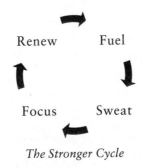

The Stronger Cycle

Chapters 1–9 focus on change at the individual level. In chapter 10, you will learn how to drive change at the team or organizational level. This final chapter provides a six-step process that any company can follow to reduce healthcare costs, to increase productivity, and to maximize the health, well-being, and performance of all its people.

Insights from Prominent Leaders

Work Stronger also features insights from private interviews that I conducted for this book with a diverse group of more than twenty-five CEOs and other highly successful people. This eclectic group includes men and women of all ages, backgrounds, and personal situations, and it includes people who work for organizations of all shapes and sizes. Insights from my interviewees are included throughout the book and are also highlighted in text boxes as "Work Stronger Wisdom."

You will learn about the beliefs and habits that are helping these people thrive. You will also learn how to take their insights and apply them to your own life, regardless of your aspirations. This book is not only for people in leadership roles. This book is for any ambitious person who wants to take their performance to a higher level.

Your Personalized Action Plan (and a Free Assessment and Workbook)

What works for someone else might not work for you. What works for you might not work for someone else. There is no single blueprint that every person must follow to enhance his or her performance or to be more successful. We do not all have the same definition of success anyway. Some of the ideas in this book will resonate with you more than others, both today and in the future.

The fact that you are reading this proves that you are open-minded and committed to becoming even better. All of us hold ourselves back in ways that we do not recognize or might not want to admit. This book will help you discover many of your blind spots, this book will help you ignite your motivation, and this book will help you transform yourself into the strongest person that you can become—physically, mentally, and psychologically.

As you will see, this book is very action oriented. Along those lines, here are three recommendations before you start chapter 1:

- **Take *The Stronger Habits Assessment* for free.** Find out how strong your habits are right now. You can take this assessment for free at WorkStronger.com. It takes less than three minutes, and you get your results immediately. You can also invite your co-workers, friends, and family to take the assessment.
- **Download a free copy of *The Work Stronger Workbook*.** This tool will help you design your personalized action plan for feeling and performing your best. You can download a free copy at WorkStronger.com.
- **Identify an accountability partner.** Any change is easier when you have someone to support you and hold you accountable along the way. Ask someone that you trust to read this book and take action with you.

You can be so much stronger than you realize. Let's get started...

Part I

THE P.O.W.E.R. PYRAMID

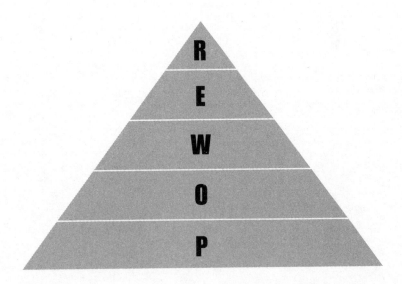

CHAPTER 1

PURPOSE

Champions are made from something they have deep inside them—a desire, a dream, a vision.

—Muhammad Ali, one of the most significant
sports figures of the twentieth century

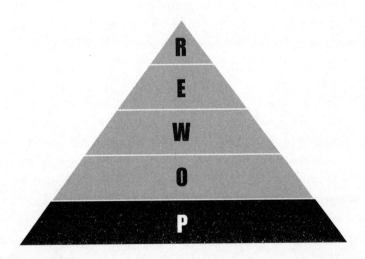

On April 6, 2007, businesswoman Arianna Huffington collapsed from exhaustion and lack of sleep. When she fell, she hit her head on the corner of her desk, spilling blood on the floor of her home office. She also broke her cheekbone and cut her eye. At the time, she was working over one hundred hours a week: this painful incident served as a major wake-up call for her.[1]

In *Thrive: The Third Metric to Redefining Success and Creating a Life of Well-Being, Wisdom, and Wonder*, Huffington writes, "In terms of the traditional measures of success, which focus on money and power, I was very successful. But I was not living a successful life by any sane definition of success. I knew something had to radically change. I could not go on that way."[2] This event propelled her to overhaul her life and to start using her influence to dismantle the widespread delusion that burnout is a price that you must pay to be successful. In addition to authoring *Thrive*, she wrote *The Sleep Revolution: Transforming Your Life, One Night at a Time.* She also launched Thrive Global in late 2016 with the mission "to end the stress and burnout epidemic."[3]

When people want to make changes, they usually begin by thinking about what to start doing or stop doing. Obviously, you need to change your behavior if you want to change your life. However, you have to change your beliefs first because your beliefs drive your behavior. Your mindset will ultimately serve as the key driver or as the key obstacle for whatever you want to achieve. In the example above, Arianna Huffington needed to change her definition of success *before* she could start living a healthier life.

Forming stronger habits can be simple and straightforward, as you will see in the chapters to follow. However, that does not mean the process will be easy. When change is tough—and it will be tough—you will consciously or subconsciously ask yourself, "Why am I doing this?"..."Why am I not eating a piece of cake when everyone else around me is?"... "Why am I exercising today instead of taking it easy at home?"..."Why am I focusing on this difficult project when I could procrastinate and work on an easier task?"..."Why am I going to bed early instead of watching TV?"

Where there is a ~~will~~ *why*, there is a way. The first level of *The P.O.W.E.R. Pyramid* is **purpose**. In this chapter, you will learn four beliefs that can drive your purpose and inspire you to make positive changes in your life.

> **Work Stronger Wisdom**
>
> "I firmly believe that the healthier you are, the more engaged you will be at work, and the more energy you will bring to every aspect of your life, not just to your career, but also to your family, your friends, and your community."
>
> —Chip Bergh, president and chief executive officer at Levi Strauss & Co., one of the world's largest brand-name apparel companies

BELIEF #1: STRONGER HABITS HELP YOU REDUCE AND PREVENT PAIN

Michael Blaue is a father who lives in Broken Arrow, Oklahoma. One day, one of his kids told him that he wanted to be like him when he grew up. He did not mention an occupation, however. Instead, his son said, "When I grow up, I'm going to be big and fat like you."[4]

This life-changing comment inspired Blaue to make some significant changes. The results were incredible—and definitely not typical. Over a ninety-day period, he lost over 18 percent of his body fat and shed over sixty pounds (going from 241 lbs. to 179 lbs.). He was also recognized as National Champion of the Golds' Gym Challenge, a twelve-week body transformation contest.[5]

If you didn't know the real story behind his makeover, you might think he just relied on willpower. However, his motivation was so much stronger. He believed that losing weight would make him a better dad. You can be certain this view helped him stay motivated on days when he was busy, tired, or not in the mood to work out or eat healthy. Now, his sons flex and do push-ups when they imitate him.[6]

A painful comment and experience is also what initially motivated me to change my body as a teenager. After my sophomore year in high school, I attended a summer basketball camp with my teammates. At the time, I was 5'10" and 119 pounds. During a break one afternoon at camp, my teammates and I were hanging out in the sun, and we were shirtless because of the heat. One of my teammates looked at me and started to laugh. "Look at Leibman," he said. "He's so puny you can see his heart beating." The entire team started cracking up. I looked down at my chest and noticed they were actually right! I tried to laugh it off though. "I don't know what you guys are talking about," I said.

It was an extremely embarrassing moment that unleashed my motivation to get stronger. I had no idea how to get started, but an older, much stronger friend named John took me under his wing. Over the next year, my body transformed. By the time I went to college, I was 6'1" and 180 pounds with less than 10 percent body fat—a significant improvement from my previously frail physique.

My reasons for forming stronger habits have certainly evolved throughout my life, but the pain of my teammate's comment was the first thing that drove me. Like Arianna Huffington and Michael Blaue, I was galvanized by what I refer to as a *Mighty Moment*, a transformational turning point that compels you to make changes. These painful experiences are the ultimate motivators.

Mighty Moments inspire many people to form stronger habits. However, you don't need to have an epiphany in order to change your behavior. If you want to reduce or prevent pain in your life, you can simply decide—at any time—to form stronger habits. To put it bluntly, you *will* experience more pain in your life without stronger habits.

One study led by Dr. Earl S. Ford of the Centers for Disease Control and Prevention in Atlanta found that a healthier lifestyle can reduce your chances of developing chronic diseases and conditions by up to 80 percent.[7] In other words, the large majority of the ailments that people experience are self-induced and preventable.

Studies have also measured the impact that specific habits can have in reducing or preventing pain associated with specific ailments. In one such study, researchers at Duke University found that exercise can be at least as effective as anti-depressant medication in treating depression.[8] Neuroscientists at the University of Georgia have also demonstrated that exercise increases galanin, a neuropeptide that contributes to stress resilience.[9]

Many people interviewed for this book highlighted stress as a key reason why they exercise and make their health and well-being a priority. One example is Barbara Tulipane, chief executive officer at National Recreation and Park Association (NRPA), the leading non-profit organization dedicated to the advancement of public parks, recreation, and conservation. "Being a CEO is a very stressful job," Barbara told me.

"You have a choice on how you can manage that stress," she says. "I see a lot of leaders who resort to alcohol. In my case, I choose to be active physically. I guess running is my 'drug of choice.' Being physically fit is a secondary benefit. To me, it's all about alleviating stress and taking care of my mental health."

BELIEF #2: STRONGER HABITS HELP YOU FEEL BETTER AND PERFORM BETTER

Countless studies have demonstrated that stronger habits in four areas (nutrition, exercise, focus, and renewal) lead to more energy and higher performance, both in the short term and the long term. Improving your behavior in these key areas will provide a multitude of benefits for your body and your brain.

Stronger eating habits (to be covered in chapter 6) improve your health, your mood, and your ability to focus. For example, a study led by Dr. Jeremy Spencer of Reading University found that something as simple as eating a large helping of blueberries (a food rich in antioxidants) could lead to increased concentration and memory up to five hours later.[10]

Stronger exercise habits (to be covered in chapter 7) make you more resilient, and MRI scans have shown that physical activity can even increase overall brain volume.[11] For example, a study performed at the University of British Columbia found that aerobic exercise can increase the size of your hippocampus, a part of the brain that is connected to learning and memory.[12]

Stronger work habits (to be covered in chapter 8) help you complete higher-quality work in less time. Research has also shown that greater focus can increase your creativity and your engagement at work. The Energy Project, a boutique consulting firm, partnered with *Harvard Business Review* in 2013 and 2014. They surveyed people globally across twenty-five industries. They found that engagement at work increased by 29 percent among those with the greatest level of focus.[13]

Stronger renewal habits (to be covered in chapter 9) make you calmer, improve your memory, and increase your attention span. For example, one study published in the *Journal of Neuroscience* looked at brain scans of regular meditators versus non-meditators. Researchers found that the meditators had greater stability in their ventral posteromedial cortex, a part of the brain associated with wandering thoughts.[14]

There is a great deal of overlap between your eating habits, exercise habits, work habits, and renewal habits. Weaker habits in any or all of these areas can send you into a downward spiral and make you feel like you are drowning. When you are not physically active, well-rested, and well-fueled, you will have less natural energy, and you will find it more difficult to focus. Many people try to compensate by fueling themselves artificially with sugary products, energy drinks, and lots of caffeine. These band-aids don't fix the problem though. They just make you more irritable and more anxious. They also make it harder to get quality sleep, and they can lead to significant health problems when consumed in excess.

In comparison, stronger habits with nutrition, exercise, focus, and renewal can propel you into an upward spiral and make you feel unstoppable—even if you are under tremendous pressure. When you are active, well-rested, and well-fueled, your energy, your mood, and your confidence skyrocket. You will also find it much easier to focus. As a result, you will produce much higher-quality output in much less time, which leaves more time for personal renewal and taking care of yourself in the future.

Stronger habits provide a rock-solid foundation for feeling and performing your best. Unfortunately, many people fail to recognize this. "A lot of people have their priorities backwards in my mind," says Frank Karbe, Chief Financial Officer at Myovant Sciences (a global biopharmaceutical company). "Health and well-being is often seen as an afterthought. In reality, you have to focus on this first because this is the source of all the energy that keeps you going with whatever you want to achieve in your career and your life."

> **Work Stronger Wisdom**
>
> "I'm more effective when I eat well. I also find that I am more balanced emotionally and sharper mentally on days when I work out in the morning. To me, this is about performance as much as it is about health and well-being."
>
> —Penny Pritzker, a triathlete, entrepreneur, civic leader, and philanthropist who also served as US Secretary of Commerce in the Obama administration

BELIEF #3: STRONGER HABITS HELP YOU THRIVE LONGER

A healthier lifestyle also enables you to thrive at work and at home for as long as possible. Just ask Dr. Larry Senn, the octogenarian chairman at Senn Delaney, a global transformational and culture-shaping organization that has worked with over one hundred Fortune 500 CEOs and their teams. While many people over the age of eighty are battling major medical issues like dementia or heart disease, Larry continues to flourish, and he does not plan on slowing down any time soon.

He recently authored *The Mood Elevator: Take Charge of Your Feelings, Become a Better You.* He still works full time, participates in action sports like jet skiing and zip-lining with his family, and competes in six triathlons a year. Actually, he doesn't just compete. He wins. He's undefeated in his age group. "Most people believe that the more hours they work and the harder they work, the more successful they will be," Larry told me. "They end up burning themselves out. I believe that by taking care of myself, I will best serve my family, and I will best serve the world."

Dr. Larry Senn, chairman at Senn Delaney

A desire to thrive longer also drives Janine Allis. Janine is the founder of Boost Juice (a juice bar company with over five hundred stores in fourteen countries, as of 2017). She is also the author of *The Accidental Entrepreneur* and an investor on *Shark Tank*. While thirty years younger than Larry, she thinks long term, too. "I know everything that I do today will affect the rest of my life," she told me. "I see little old ladies with wheelchairs and canes. That's not going to be me."

When discussing the playing careers of athletes, ESPN commentator Michael Wilbon has said that "Father Time is undefeated."[15] Eventually, Father Time will beat all of us. It is up to you how soon and how easily that happens though.

Work Stronger Wisdom

"It's impossible to have longevity in your professional career without taking care of yourself. You need to realize the finish line for your career is very far away."

—Alex Douzet, an Ironman finisher and a serial entrepreneur whose ventures have included co-founding Ollie (a trailblazing pet wellness brand) and TheLadders.com (a career resource now used by more than eight million professionals)

Alex Douzet, serial entrepreneur

BELIEF #4: STRONGER HABITS MAKE YOU A STRONGER LEADER AND ROLE MODEL

In a controversial Nike commercial in 1993, then NBA All-Star (and now Hall of Famer) Charles Barkley boldly declared, "I am not a role model. I am not paid to be a role model."[16] Regardless of Barkley's intentions, the ad struck a chord with many people. The media went wild, and many parents were outraged by his comments.

Shortly after the ad first ran, another NBA All-Star at the time (and also now a Hall of Famer), Karl "The Mailman" Malone, wrote a column for *Sports Illustrated* that was directed at Charles' comments. As he wrote, "...Charles, you can deny being a role model all you want, but I don't think it's your decision to make. We don't choose to be role models, we are chosen. Our only choice is whether to be a good role model or a bad one."[17]

This message does not only apply to famous athletes. It applies to each of us, especially as more and more of our lives are on display through social media. We are all role models. This is even more relevant for parents and for people in leadership roles at work. Your behavior influences everyone around you—in good ways or bad ways.

Leaders at work have a major impact on the beliefs, behavior, and performance of the people around them. Laurie Coe, managing director of Organizational Consulting at The Energy Project, says, "We tell leaders, 'You are the Chief Energy Officer. You have a disproportionate impact on the energy of everyone around you because everyone is watching you. When you take care of yourself and manage your own energy, you show people that this is important, *and* you also give your employees permission to do the same. You don't need to be perfect. But you do need to be mindful of it and start by taking responsibility for yourself.'"

The desire to be a stronger leader and role model came up repeatedly during my interviews for this book, including my conversation with Hoby Darling. Hoby was previously the CEO at Skullcandy, a creator of world-class audio and gaming products. Before that, he was a GM at Nike. "I believe that a big part of my job is to inspire other people to be great both in their personal and professional lives," he told me. "This [a healthy lifestyle] is so important. It makes you a better leader, it makes you a better parent, it makes you a better friend. When you look at it that way, you think 'how could you not find time for this?' As a leader, there are no bad days. Everyone is looking at you. You set the tone."

> **Work Stronger Wisdom**
> "You have to take care of yourself first if you want to take care of other people as a leader."
> —Rhonda Vetere, chief technology officer at Estée Lauder Companies, one of the world's leading manufacturers and marketers of quality skin care, makeup, fragrance, and hair care products

CHAPTER SUMMARY

The first level of *The P.O.W.E.R. Pyramid* is purpose. Where there is a ~~will~~ *why*, there is a way. This chapter highlighted four beliefs that can drive your purpose and inspire you to make positive changes in your life:

- Belief #1: Stronger habits help you reduce and prevent pain.
- Belief #2: Stronger habits help you feel better and perform better.
- Belief #3: Stronger habits help you thrive longer.
- Belief #4: Stronger habits make you a stronger leader and role model.

Before you think about *how* to change your behavior, make sure you are clear on *why* you want to change. When change feels difficult, remind yourself why you started and why you should continue. Here are some questions that you might want to ask yourself as you reflect on this chapter:

- How often do you feel like you are at your best at work and at home? How might your life improve if you form stronger habits in regard to nutrition, exercise, focus, and renewal?
- How are you trending in regard to your health, your energy, and your stress? What will your life look like in the future if you continue at your current rate?
- Who matters most to you? What kind of example are you setting for these people with your current habits?

CHAPTER 2

OPTIMISM

The greatest discovery of all time is that a person can change by merely changing his attitude.
—Oprah Winfrey, a global media leader, philanthropist, producer, and actress

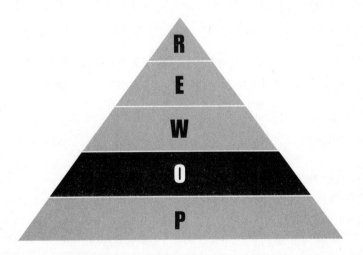

In the 1950s, there were two primary groups of inhabitants living in a small village on the southern tip of Trinidad, an island located about seven miles off the northeastern coast of Venezuela. One group was of East Indian descent and one was of African descent. Each group lived peacefully on different sides of the village.

Dr. Walter Mischel, a graduate student at the time, spent one summer in Trinidad living near this small village. He noticed that adults from each group had a contrasting stereotype about the self-control of the other group. The East Indians perceived the Africans to be more impulsive and eager to live in the moment, without thinking about or planning for the future. In contrast, the Africans perceived the East Indians to always be working and slaving away for the future, without ever really enjoying the present.

These opposing perceptions piqued Dr. Mischel's curiosity. He wanted to evaluate if the stereotypes were really accurate. So, he went to the local school, which was attended by children from each of the two groups, and he got permission to run a small experiment on those aged eleven to fourteen from each group. Dr. Mischel asked each of the children who lived in their homes. He also assessed each child's intelligence and motivation, among other factors. At the end of each of his sessions, he gave each child a choice between having a small piece of chocolate immediately, or having a much larger piece of chocolate the following week. The children were also asked to choose between receiving ten dollars immediately, or receiving thirty dollars if they waited a month. Finally, each child was offered a "much larger gift much later or a smaller one now."

Dr. Mischel ultimately found that the stereotypes he had heard from/about each of the two groups were generally accurate. Children from the African group generally opted for the rewards immediately, while children from the East Indian group generally chose to wait for a larger reward in the future. Dr. Mischel thought there was more to the story, though. He hypothesized that children who came from homes with absent fathers (something much more common at the time among the African group) had fewer experiences with men who kept their promises. Therefore, he believed that such children would have less trust that a stranger like him would follow through on a promise to deliver a larger reward in the future. After he factored this into consideration, he found that the differences between the groups disappeared.

In *The Marshmallow Test: Understanding Self-Control and How to Master It*, Dr. Mischel discusses this experiment (and many others) on how people decide between smaller, immediate rewards and larger, delayed rewards. As he writes when explaining his time in Trinidad, "There's no good reason for anyone to forgo the 'now' unless there is trust that the 'later' will materialize...When people don't expect delayed rewards to be delivered, they behave rationally and won't choose to wait for them."[1]

In other words, if you do not believe that there will be a future payoff for delaying short-term gratification, then you are acting rationally by choosing the outcome that is in your best interest in the short term. If you do what feels good in the moment more often than you would like, you might think this is happening because you lack willpower. However, your real problem might be the way that you are thinking about the present and your future.

Dr. Mischel expands on this theme later in his book. As he writes, "Because optimists have higher overall expectations of success, they are more willing to delay gratification, even when it is difficult to do so... Our broad expectations of success or failure crucially impact how we approach new tasks, but our specific expectations are responsive to change when we see that we can actually succeed. The message is clear: optimists in general are better off than pessimists, but even pessimists raise their expectations when they see that they can succeed."[2]

The second level of *The P.O.W.E.R. Pyramid* is **optimism**. In this chapter, you will learn three strategies for developing a positive outlook, so that you can increase your chances of success for whatever you want to change or achieve.

STRATEGY #1: ADOPT A "GROWTH MINDSET" FOR YOUR HABITS

For decades, Stanford University psychologist Dr. Carol S. Dweck has studied the relationship between mindset and success. The central theme of her work is that people can have one of two mindsets. You can either have a "fixed mindset," in which you believe that your abilities are fixed, or you can have a "growth mindset," in which you believe that your abilities can be developed.

People with a fixed mindset avoid challenges (to avoid a potential failure), or they view setbacks and criticism as evidence that they lack a certain skill or positive trait. On the other hand, people with a growth mindset pursue challenges (even though they might fail), and they use setbacks and criticism as evidence that they should try a new approach or work harder to improve their results in the future. To be clear, you can have a growth mindset in certain ways and a fixed mindset in other ways. For example, you could have a growth mindset in regard to your leadership ability, while having a fixed mindset in regard to your ability to get up early or to lose weight.

As Dr. Dweck writes in *Mindset: The New Psychology of Success*, "For twenty years, my research has shown that the view you adopt for yourself profoundly affects the way you lead your life. It can determine whether you become the person you want to be and whether you accomplish the things you value."[3]

She continues with a question, "Do people with this [growth] mindset believe that anyone can be anything, that anyone with proper motivation or education can become Einstein or Beethoven? No, but they believe that a person's true potential is unknown (and unknowable); that it's impossible to foresee what can be accomplished with years of passion, toil, and training."[4]

Where Might You Be Holding Yourself Back with a Fixed Mindset?

A fixed mindset is often displayed through the words that we use to describe ourselves. We often hold ourselves back with pessimistic, artificial thoughts and excuses that may or may not really be true. This includes what we are or are not, e.g., "I'm not a morning person" or "I'm not good at ___" or "I'm too old to ___." This also includes what we have or don't have, e.g., "I have a slow metabolism" or "I don't have any willpower" or "I don't have time to ___." In addition, this includes what we cannot do, e.g., "I cannot lose weight" or "I cannot enjoy exercise" or "I cannot stop ___."

The labels, identities, and excuses that you assign to yourself (or that you allow others to assign to you) have a powerful impact on your behavior. Be very careful with how you view yourself and how you speak about yourself. When you tell yourself that you are "not a morning person," you will behave like someone who is "not a morning person," and you will have more trouble getting out of bed and starting your day strong. When you tell yourself that you "don't have any willpower," you will behave like someone who lacks willpower, and you will eat more junk food. When you tell yourself that you "cannot enjoy exercise," you will behave like someone who does not enjoy exercise, and you will be less likely to work out.

How Can You Develop a Growth Mindset?

Begin by identifying where you have a fixed mindset. Then, ask yourself how your beliefs might not really be accurate. For example, if you think that you are "not a morning person," you might have years of evidence that seem to support your belief. However, chances are that your morning struggles are simply due to your sleep environment and what you are doing and not doing before you go to bed. A stronger morning really begins the night before. (More to come on this specific example in chapter 9.)

As another example, I once spoke with an executive who told me that he had a slow metabolism. He believed this was a genetic issue and the reason why he was overweight. I asked him how much he exercised and how much strength training he did. (As we will discuss in chapter 7, strength training is one of the best ways to increase your metabolism and improve your body composition.) He told me that he rarely exercised and never did strength training. Well, guess what? You should not be surprised if you have a slow metabolism and are overweight if you rarely exercise and never do strength training. Your situation is not fixed just because you have evidence (i.e., being overweight) that appears to support a fixed mindset belief (i.e., "I have a slow metabolism").

As Dr. Dweck's research has shown, different beliefs lead to different behaviors and different results. A desire to change (purpose) is not sufficient. You also have to believe that you can change. Why not adopt a growth mindset for all of your behavior and for every area of your life?

STRATEGY #2: FOLLOW THE HEADLIGHTS METHOD

In 2009, I left a full-time job to launch a career as a keynote speaker and to write a book for students on how to go from college to career. Most people advising students are much older. I believed that students would be able to relate to me more easily, because I was a young man in my late twenties at that time.

After diving into my venture with passion and purpose, I quickly felt overwhelmed and got off to a rough start. Six months in, I had not even written a single article or shared any of my ideas publicly. All of my effort had been spent brainstorming and completing research. At the time, I told myself this was a necessary step in the writing process. In reality, it was a stall tactic due to a fear of putting myself out there and sharing my ideas with the world. My behavior was also a side effect of pursuing a goal (writing a book for students) that was very exciting to me, yet one that felt "too big."

Something had to change, so I decided to break down my big goal into a "small" weekday habit: writing (and posting) one three- to five-hundred-word article online every day, Monday to Friday. This became my new focus. The goal of writing a book was moved to the back of my mind. My early articles were not very impressive. Looking back now at some of those articles makes me cringe. However, they helped me get started. My writing got better over time, and my weekday habit eventually led to a contract for what became my first book, *I Got My Dream Job and So Can You*.

The late Edgar Lawrence "E.L." Doctorow, one of the most successful American novelists of the twentieth century, once said that, "Writing is like driving at night in the fog. You can only see as far as your headlights, but you can make the whole trip that way."5

This is a great metaphor to keep in mind for any challenge in life. While big goals can be energizing and can help make life exciting, they can also feel overwhelming, either right away or after you get started. Do not allow yourself to feel paralyzed by the magnitude of what you are trying to accomplish. Instead, tighten your attention, and look only as far as "your headlights." Break down your big goal into tangible, bite-sized habits that you can repeat over and over. I refer to this as *the Headlights Method*. Chapters 6–9 will help you apply *the Headlights Method* by highlighting specific, scalable behaviors that will increase your energy, decrease your stress, and take your performance to a higher level.

The strategy of breaking down a big goal is a topic that came up during my interview with Tom Lokar. Tom is a triathlete, and he is the chief human resources officer at Mitel, a global leader in enterprise business communications. "People put off change for lots of reasons," Tom told me. "I think it's largely because they look too far out and feel overwhelmed. Just get through day one. Don't look three months out. It is so critical to give yourself a pat on the back for getting through day one. If you can get through the first day, you can get through the next five days, the next ten days, the next thirty days, and so on."

Tom Lokar, CHRO at Mitel

You can increase your motivation—especially when you are getting started—by focusing on small habits along the way, instead of thinking about how far you have to go to reach your ideal destination. It's better to smart small and build positive momentum than to bite off more than you can chew and feel overwhelmed from the start. Focus on getting some early wins to boost your optimism and confidence. Look only as far as your headlights. You can expand any habit (or add on another new one) later.

How can you tell if a behavior change is the right size for you (i.e., if you are only looking as far as your headlights)? Ask yourself how confident you are that you could do it every day or most days. If you are less than 90 percent confident, take that as a sign to reduce the size of the behavior.[6]

STRATEGY #3: FIND A RELEVANT ROLE MODEL

It was 5:30 p.m. on a Tuesday night in July. I arrived at Clean and Sober Streets (CSS), a homeless shelter in Washington, D.C. that has provided free services to over five thousand men and women since 1987. The majority of these people, like most who are homeless, have battled drug and alcohol addictions. I was there that night to celebrate the one-year sobriety anniversary for a man named Gary who I got to know through my work as a volunteer with Back on My Feet (BOMF). BOMF is a non-profit organization that part-ners with shelters like CSS to help homeless people improve their lives physically and emotionally. The organization uses running and community to motivate and support people from homelessness to independence.[7]

Over one hundred people gathered that night to celebrate with Gary. This army of supporters included BOMF volunteers and staff, in addition to some of Gary's friends and family. However, most of the people in the room were other men and women at various stages of addiction and recovery. Several speakers, including Gary, shared their journey with the group that night. Each person was honest, vulnerable, and uncensored. At some point, each individual said, "I felt hopeless." However, each story ended on a positive, as each person had achieved and maintained sobriety. The stories were not the only inspiring part of the event though.

At one point, Brian, the person running the meeting, asked, "Who has been sober for one day to one month?" A group of people stood up. You could see the apprehensiveness in their eyes. Then, Brian asked, "Who has been sober for one month to three months?" Another group of people stood up. Then, he asked who had been sober for three months to six months. Then, he asked who had been sober for six months to twelve months. The crowd cheered each time people stood up. The individuals seemed to stand taller and prouder as the sobriety streaks got longer.

Brian continued…"Who has been sober for two years to three years?"…"for three years to four years?"…"for four years to five years?"…Brian eventually went all the way up to recognize an alcoholic who had been sober for over forty years.

There were twenty to thirty people there that night who had been sober for anywhere from one day to thirty days. Imagine being one of those people. You may have battled a crippling addiction for years. The path to sobriety could easily feel impossible. Then, you see over fifty people who used to be like you, yet who have achieved and maintained sobriety for months, years, or even decades. Even the most hopeless person would have to wonder, "If all of these people overcame this addiction, why can't I do the same?"

Clearly, anyone battling an addiction has a difficult road ahead. An experience like this would not eliminate any future feelings of hopelessness. However, with repeated exposure to this sort of community, support, and evidence, many get their lives back on track. There is a powerful lesson here for anyone who wants to achieve change in their lives, no matter how big or small. The most powerful way to increase your optimism is to find what I refer to as a *Relevant Role Model*. This is someone who used to be like you (the more like you, the better), but who overcame similar or even bigger obstacles to get where you want to be. You can find such a person by doing research online, or by asking people that you trust if they know anyone who has done what you hope to achieve. This will take some time and effort, but it's definitely worth it.

Change is not easy. You will have doubts. You will have setbacks. You will have moments when you want to give up. You need a strong sense of optimism that you can succeed. Without tangible, personal proof that change is possible for someone like you, even the most determined person can lose hope and motivation. When you know of someone like you who overcame similar or larger obstacles, you know there is no reason why you cannot achieve similar results. A *Relevant Role Model* shifts your mindset from "I don't know if I can succeed" to "*I know* I can succeed, because someone like me succeeded too."

IT'S NEVER TOO LATE TO CHANGE

At her unhealthiest point, Rhonda Germany-Ballintyn weighed over two hundred pounds, while being 5'2". Rhonda is retired now, after having served most recently as chief strategy and marketing officer at Honeywell, a Fortune 100 software-industrial company. "I was very, very heavy for a lot of years," Rhonda told me. "I had two kids while I was a partner at Booz Allen Hamilton, and I was traveling the world and working one hundred hours a week."

In 2010, Rhonda decided it was finally time to start taking better care of herself. She didn't want to become "one of those old ladies who falls and breaks her hip and has to walk around with a walker." So, she started paying more attention to what she was eating. She also started lifting weights at a modest gym that catered to overweight women.

> **Work Stronger Wisdom**
> "Think about how you can, rather than why you can't."
> —Bahram Akradi, chairman, CEO, and founder
> of Life Time®, the Healthy Way
> of Life Company

The pounds started to come off, and she quickly grew out of her first gym and initial workout regimen, moving on to one that was more advanced. Actually, it would be more accurate to say that she "shrunk out of" her first gym. Rhonda's body transformed and she eventually lost over one hundred pounds.

Today, Rhonda is stronger and healthier than ever. The year before this book was published, she told me that she was planning to get certified as a fitness trainer, so that she could serve as a healthy role model for other people struggling with weight management. "I feel good all the time now," Rhonda said. "It's amazing how much stronger and fitter I am. I feel at sixty years old that I can do anything. This has given me a lot more confidence for going after what I want post-retirement."

CHAPTER SUMMARY

The second level of *The P.O.W.E.R. Pyramid* is optimism. It's never too late to change. You *can* teach an old dog new tricks, as long as the dog has a purpose for learning new tricks and is optimistic that it can. When you want to change (purpose) and believe that you can change (optimism), you will have the mindset required to change or achieve anything. This chapter highlighted three strategies for developing a positive outlook:

- Strategy #1: Adopt a "growth mindset" for your habits
- Strategy #2: Follow *the Headlights Method*
- Strategy #3: Find a *Relevant Role Model*

Here are some questions that you might want to ask yourself as you reflect on this chapter:

- Where might you be holding yourself back with a fixed mindset? How could you challenge these beliefs and develop more of a growth mindset?
- Think of a goal that feels overwhelming to you. How could you follow *the Headlights Method* to make this goal feel more achievable?
- Who could you look at as a *Relevant Role Model* for a goal that you would like to achieve?

CHAPTER 3

THE WAY

Our prototypical model of self-control is angel on one side and devil on the other, and they battle it out. We tend to think of people with strong willpower as people who are able to fight this battle effectively. Actually, the people who are really good at self-control never have these battles in the first place.
—Dr. Kentaro Fujita, a psychologist at the Ohio State University who studies self-control[1]

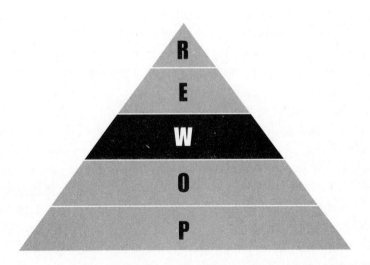

Leading up to the 1998 Draft for the National Football League (NFL), the top two prospects were Peyton Manning out of the University of Tennessee and Ryan Leaf out of Washington State University. Both men were twenty-two years old, both played quarterback, and both were 6'5" and about 230 pounds. Both had outstanding college careers and were viewed by most prognosticators as "can't miss" prospects.

Leaf seemed to have a stronger arm, more natural ability, and higher upside. Manning seemed to be more mature and a safer choice, however. With the first pick, the Indianapolis Colts selected Manning. The San Diego Chargers then chose Leaf with the second pick. The impact of these selections cannot be overstated.

Manning went on to become one of the greatest quarterbacks in NFL history. He played in 266 NFL games in an illustrious career, throwing for 71,940 passing yards and 539 touchdown passes.[2] He made the Pro Bowl fourteen times, was recognized as the NFL's Most Valuable Player (MVP) five times, and won the Super Bowl twice.[3] Off the field, he became one of the NFL's most marketable players, and he was invited to host *Saturday Night Live* on multiple occasions.

Leaf went on to become one of the biggest busts in NFL history. He only played in twenty-five NFL games in a tumultuous career, throwing for just 3,666 passing yards and fourteen touchdown passes.[4] He never made the Pro Bowl, was never recognized as the NFL's MVP, and never won the Super Bowl. Off the field, he battled drug and legal problems, and he was forced to spend time in prison.[5] (Leaf eventually turned his life around. He became an author and motivational speaker dedicated to helping young adults avoid the mistakes that cost him his career.[6])

Two gifted athletes with similar talent had vastly different careers and lives. How did this happen? Sure, Manning had a psychological makeup that was better suited to the NFL. He was much more resilient and much less volatile than Leaf. Manning's family didn't hurt either. His father, Archie, and brother, Eli, both played in the NFL as well. However, those factors didn't cause the huge chasm between the careers of these two men. They contributed to the variable that made the difference: *habits*.

Manning's habits as a pro became legendary. The week after being drafted, he memorized the Colts' entire playbook. In the two weeks leading up to Super Bowl XLI (played in 2007 between the Colts and the Chicago Bears), he studied all eighteen games the Bears had played that year in the regular season and post-season. He also had his backup (quarterback Jim Sorgi) study all four of the Bears' preseason games and then report back to him—just in case the Bears used any different defenses in the preseason.[7]

Leaf's habits as a pro became the stuff of legend too, but for the opposite reason. The night after being drafted by the Chargers, he flew to Las Vegas and partied all night.[8] During his career, he reportedly missed practices to play golf.[9]

You become what you repeat. The third level of *The P.O.W.E.R. Pyramid* is **the way**. In this chapter, you will see how habits form, and you will also learn practical strategies on the way to break habits and on the way to make habits. Different strategies are required for each kind of change.

HOW HABITS FORM

When people decide they want to form stronger habits, they often just try to stop or start a certain behavior. Just trying to have more willpower is rarely effective because habits do not occur in a vacuum. In *The Power of Habit: Why We Do What We Do in Life and Business*, Charles Duhigg shares a framework on how our brains form habits. He refers to this process as "The Habit Loop."[10]

As Duhigg writes, "This process within our brains is a three-step loop. First, there is a *cue*, a trigger that tells your brain to go into automatic mode and which habit to use. Then, there is the *routine*, which can be physical or mental or emotional. Finally, there is a *reward*, which helps you figure out if this particular loop is worth remembering for the future…. Over time, this loop—cue, routine, reward; cue, routine, reward—becomes more and more automatic. The cue and reward become intertwined until a powerful sense of anticipation and craving emerges."[11]

While bad habits provide dangerous or even deadly consequences over the long term, they form because of the rewards they provide in the short term. Habits—both the good kind and the bad kind—get stronger and stronger as you begin to yearn for the reward at the end of the loop. That is essential. The cue and reward are not sufficient on their own. As Duhigg writes, "Cravings are what drive habits. And figuring out how to spark a craving makes creating a new habit easier...every morning, millions put on their jogging shoes to capture an endorphin rush they've learned to crave."[12]

If you eat a lot of junk food or snooze every morning, it is not because you lack willpower. It is because you have succumbed to the dark side of "The Habit Loop" that all of our brains are governed by. If you eat a lot of kale or crush it at the gym at 6:00 a.m. each morning, it is also not because of willpower. It is because of the bright side of "The Habit Loop" that all of our brains are governed by. Our brains form habits as a way to conserve energy. That way, you do not have to think about how to tie your shoes, how to brush your teeth, how to drive a car, and so on.

To be clear, you don't have to eat kale or exercise before work if you don't want to. That's not the point. The message is that virtually every behavior—good or bad—is simply part of a process that you can change.

HOW TO BREAK ANY HABIT

The first step in breaking a habit is to identify the routine (the habit) that you want to break, the cue(s) that serve as a trigger, and the short-term reward(s) that entice you to perform the behavior. Cues can be visual, emotional, mental, physical, or social. Another action or a certain day or time can also be a cue. Here are some examples of habit loops for negative behaviors:

- You see candy on your desk (visual cue), so you eat the treat (routine) in order to enjoy something sweet (reward).
- You feel stressed (emotional cue), so you smoke a cigarette (routine) in order to feel relaxed (reward).
- You are bored (mental cue), so you scroll through Facebook (routine) in order to receive intellectual stimulation (reward).
- You are tired (physical cue), so you consume an artificial energy drink (routine) in order to have more energy (reward).
- Your friends stay out until 2:00 a.m. drinking alcohol on a weekend (social cue), so you drink with them and stay up

late as well (routine) in order to feel like part of the group (reward).

- It's the weekend (time-based cue), so you eat a huge ice cream sundae (routine) in order to enjoy something cold, sweet, and creamy (reward).

Once you understand the individual components in an unhealthy habit loop, you can utilize one of the following three strategies for breaking a bad habit. This does not mean that change will be easy or that change will happen quickly. However, you will be clear on what you need to do.

Strategy #1: Remove or Reduce the Cue

Research led by Dr. Wilhelm Hofmann of the University of Cologne has found that, on average, we feel some sort of desire about half of the time that we are awake, and almost half of those desires conflict with our goals, values, or motivations.[13] Rather than waste time and energy trying to resist the endless forms of temptation that surround us in today's world, why not try to remove some of them altogether?

This is easiest to do with visual cues, like candy on your desk. You can often remove other cues though as well. As an example, consider the bad habit of drinking an artificial energy drink. Better fuel (more to come on that in chapter 6) and better sleep (more to come on that in chapter 9) might remove or reduce the cue of feeling exhausted, thereby decreasing the craving for a routine that helps you feel more energetic.

Other bad habits can be broken by reducing your exposure to the cue. For example, consider the late-night drinking habit above. By socializing less often with certain people (or by socializing with them at different times or at different venues), you could cut back on alcohol consumption and late nights that reduce your sleep quality and your overall energy.

Much of what is believed about willpower and self-control has been disproven by recent scientific research. In one experiment conducted by Dr. Hofmann, researchers gave 205 participants Black-Berrys that would go off at random. During those times, participants were asked about temptations, desires, and self-control that they were currently experiencing. The research discovered an interesting finding. The people who said they were the best at self-control reported fewer temptations during the course of the study. In other words, the people who said they were the best at self-control were the ones who were testing their self-control the least.[14]

Strategy #2: Swap or Shrink the Routine

For those cues that you cannot remove or reduce, your best strategy is to prepare a better way to respond. Many behaviors can be swapped out for healthier options. The key here is to decide in advance (not in the heat of the moment) how you will respond if you experience a cue that usually triggers a bad habit. Here are three examples from the habit loops highlighted earlier in this chapter:

- When you feel stressed, you will go for a walk (instead of smoking a cigarette) in order to feel relaxed.
- When you are bored, you will read an educational book (instead of scrolling through your Facebook page) in order to receive intellectual stimulation.
- When it is the weekend, you will eat a healthier, homemade ice cream with 100 percent coconut water and frozen bananas (instead of a huge, artificially processed ice cream sundae) in order to enjoy something cold, sweet, and creamy.

Of course, another option is to shrink your bad habit, instead of swapping it out altogether. Instead of eating three scoops of ice cream, you could eat one. Instead of eating an entire pizza, you could eat two slices. Instead of drinking six beers, you could drink three. You could gradually reduce the size of a bad habit over time. Or, you could shrink the behavior once, so it has a smaller impact.

Strategy #3: Reframe the Reward

In a study led by Dr. Hedy Kober, heavy cigarette smokers were shown photographs of cigarettes to induce cravings. One group of participants was instructed to think about its immediate, short-term effect (i.e., "it will feel good"), while the other group was instructed to think about the long-term consequences (i.e., "I may get lung cancer"). Researchers found that focusing on the latter led to a significant reduction in cigarette cravings.[15]

Dr. Walter Mischel discusses this study in *The Marshmallow Test*. As he writes, "we found that people can use simple cognitive strategies to regulate their cravings by shifting their time perspective from 'now' to 'later.'"[16] He also refers to this as "cooling the now and heating the later."[17] In other words, if you experience a craving that you want to avoid, you can reduce your chances of giving in by focusing on the long-term costs, instead of the short-term benefits.

Will reframing the reward immediately help you stop doing any unhealthy behavior for good? Of course not. However, this can be another method used to break bad habits over time.

The strategy of reframing the reward came up during my conversation with Dr. Larry Senn, the vibrant octogenarian discussed in chapter 1. Larry has an interesting tactic to avoid junk food when it is in his sight. "When I see a cookie, I see my [seventeen-year-old] son Logan's face on it, and I don't eat it," he told me. As this example demonstrates, Larry is not focused on what he would gain in the short term by indulging: brief pleasure for his taste buds. He is focused on what he believes he would lose in the long term by indulging: time with his son.

Many short-term rewards provide gratification that is immediate, but brief and largely unsatisfying. Many also come with what I refer to as a *Gratification Cost*. For example, every time you smoke a cigarette, eat a cookie, waste time on social media, or engage in other low-value or harmful activities, there is a price to pay. You decide to move a little further away from feeling and performing your best. This does not mean that every second of your life needs to be productive and healthy. This simply means that life is a series of tradeoffs.

You can have small rewards now (usually with negative consequences later), or you can delay short-term gratification and enjoy much bigger rewards later. To say it another way, you can "live a little" by giving in to short-term temptations, or you can "live a lot" by delaying immediate gratification for bigger, more positive outcomes in the future.

HOW TO MAKE ANY HABIT STICK

Now that we have discussed how to break a habit, let's discuss three strategies on the way to make a habit:

Strategy #1: Hook the Habit

The first strategy to make a new habit stick is to "hook" it onto an existing routine or activity. Credit for this term goes to Brendon Burchard in his book *The Charge: Activating the 10 Human Drives That Make You Feel Alive.*[18] You can hook a new habit onto another action that you already do every day or on certain days. Here are six examples:

- Your morning routine
- Your commute to work
- Your lunch hour
- Your commute home after work
- Your bedtime routine
- Your meals

You could also hook a new habit onto any other activity that you do often, such as showering, brushing your teeth, checking your email, shopping for food, doing laundry, cooking, and so on. Here are three of the countless examples of how you could put this strategy into practice to make a new habit stick:

- If you want to form the habit of stretching, you could hook this new habit onto your morning routine.
- If you want to form the habit of drinking more water, you could hook this new habit onto one or more of your meals.
- If you want to form the habit of meditating each day, you could hook this new habit onto your bedtime routine.

To further increase your chances of making your new habit stick, you could also use a post-it note as a visual reminder. For example, you could place a post-it note on your nightstand as a reminder to meditate before bed.

A twist on hooking a behavior is to *hide* the behavior when you experience a larger change in your life, such as moving to a new city, starting a new job, becoming a parent, or getting married. You might find that a new habit feels like less of a shock and is easier to adopt when it is hidden inside of a larger transition, instead of being implemented during a more stable period. In an experiment led by Dr. Todd F. Heatherton of Dartmouth College, people trying to make various changes in their lives were studied. Researchers found that over 35 percent of successful changes were associated with a move to a new location.[19]

Strategy # 2: Predict and Overcome Obstacles

Some people encounter challenges and use them as excuses to abandon a good habit. A stronger approach is to anticipate obstacles in advance and determine how you will overcome them. While it might sound pessimistic to think about everything that could get in the way of forming a new habit, this step is crucial. It increases your commitment and your likelihood of success in making a habit stick.

For example, let's say that you want to form the habit of starting each day with a natural, nutrient-dense breakfast (which we will discuss in more detail in chapter 6). Two of the obstacles that you could face in forming and keeping this habit are (1) lacking the necessary ingredients and cooking tools in your home and (2) lacking time in the morning to prepare and eat the meal. You could easily overcome these obstacles, however, by purchasing ingredients and cooking tools in advance, by getting up a little earlier, and/or by preparing/purchasing part or all of your breakfasts in advance.

While this example might seem obvious and basic, few people step back and design a strategy on the way that they will make a new habit stick. Asking yourself what could get in the way, and thinking about how you will overcome those potential obstacles will dramatically increase your chances of making your desired behavior last. Poor planning (not a lack of willpower or discipline) is the real cause of many failed attempts at forming new habits.

Strategy # 3: Tweak the Routine

Have you ever used boredom or a perceived plateau as excuses to abandon a good habit? There are two stronger approaches. First of all, don't allow yourself to get bored or to feel like you are stagnating. Secondly, if you do experience monotony or perceived lack of progress, use those feelings as signals to tweak your routines, not as signals to ditch them. Minor modifications can keep a routine fresh, make a habit stick, and lead to better results.

For example, let's say that you want to form the habit of exercising before every workday. There are many ways that you could tweak your exercise habit so that it lasts for weeks, months, and years. You could exercise at different locations, with different exercises, with different people, with different equipment, with different music, or with different trainers. (More to come on all of this in chapter 7.) You could also mix it up by raising the bar and working out at a higher intensity. Or, you might need to lower the bar at times, either because you bit off more than you could chew and the "size" of a habit feels too big, or because of other priorities in your life.

The strategy of tweaking routines came up during my conversation with Dr. Josh Riff, CEO at Onduo, a joint venture launched in fall 2016 between Sanofi and Verily Life Sciences (formerly Google Life Sciences), an Alphabet company. Before Onduo, Josh's roles included serving as senior vice president of prevention and well-being for Optum and serving as chief medical director for Target. In his free time, Josh has competed in ultramarathons, cross country skiing marathons, and other extreme endurance challenges.

Josh's typical workout schedule includes forty-five to sixty minutes of exercise at least five days a week. However, he adjusts this throughout the year. "I'm a big believer in periodization and prioritization," he told me. "There are times in the year when I'll only work out a few times a week for enjoyment. There are other times leading up to a race when I'm more focused. You have to be able to take your training up and down, based on what's going on in your family, your career, your overall health, and so on."

Research has demonstrated that tweaking your routine helps with habit formation. In one study led by Dr. Christopher Janelle of the University of Florida, volunteers were divided into three groups. One group was required to perform the same exercise program for eight weeks, a second group was given a program that featured variety, and the third group was not given any specific directions. As expected, people in the group with the varied program were significantly more likely to stick to the program, and they reported higher enjoyment levels as well.[20]

> **Work Stronger Wisdom**
> "You don't have to make big changes overnight. Small changes can have a huge impact on your health, well-being, and performance in the long run. Over time, you can end up on a completely different trajectory."
>
> —Frank Karbe, an executive recognized in 2005 and 2013 by CEO Challenges as "World's Fittest CEO"

FOCUS ON YOUR FUTURE SELF

Leading up to the filming of *Hercules*, Dwayne "The Rock" Johnson followed an exercise program that included 4:00 a.m. workouts and more than ten hours of intense training each week. He also followed a very rigid nutrition program for six months that consisted of seven strict meals and over 5,000 precise calories a day.[21]

How did he follow this rigorous program for months? Did he just try to rely on willpower? No, he focused on who he wanted to become—the best Hercules of all time. He motivated himself with what I refer to as an *Inspiring Identity*, a greater vision of yourself that compels you to adopt stronger habits. One way to take your life to a higher level is by envisioning a stronger version of yourself first, whatever that vision might be for you. An *Inspiring Identity* will help you reach a level that you would otherwise never access.

If you are not focused on your future self, then of course you will give in to the endless sources of short-term gratification that surround you in today's world. Smaller, immediate prizes become irresistible when you don't have your eyes on bigger, delayed prizes, like an *Inspiring Identity*. You could think, "Well, it's easy for someone like Dwayne Johnson to think the way that he does. He's 'The Rock.'" Perhaps, but maybe he's the "The Rock" we all know *because* of how he thinks. It is certainly not because life has always been easy for him.

You might just think of Johnson as a charming, musclebound celebrity. What you might not know is that he had a chaotic childhood that included run-ins with the law and moving homes more than ten times. When he was fourteen years old, he came home one day and found an eviction notice on the door to the unit where he and his mother were living at the time. The week before that, his mother's car had also been repossessed. He failed to achieve his first dream (to be a professional football player) and has battled depression several times throughout his life, including in 2008 when he went through a painful divorce.[22] Maybe part of the reason why "The Rock" has become one of the biggest "rags-to-riches" stories of all time is because of the ever-evolving identity that he has envisioned for himself along the way.

While the strategy of thinking about your future self is a little more abstract than the other strategies in this chapter, it's a really powerful way to break bad habits *and* make good habits stick. Research has demonstrated that the more emotionally connected you are to your future self, the more that you will make decisions based on your long-term interest.

For example, in one experiment led by Dr. Hal Hershfield, researchers studied a group of college students as they made financial decisions. Before the experiment began, the students submitted a photo of themselves. Then, the researchers created an avatar (a digital representation) of each photo. For some of the students, the avatar was of the student at his or her current age. For other students, the avatar was adjusted to represent what the students might look like at the age of sixty-eight.[23]

During the experiment, students indicated what percentage of a hypothetical paycheck they would allocate for retirement (future reward) and what percentage they would allocate for take-home pay (immediate reward). Each student's avatar (either a current or future version) appeared on the computer screen while they completed this exercise. Students who were shown an older avatar indicated that they would save 30 percent more than students who were shown an avatar of their current self.[24]

HOW LONG DOES IT REALLY TAKE TO FORM A NEW HABIT?

This is a very common question that is unfortunately impossible to answer. There are many factors that influence the speed of behavior change, including your mindset, the complexity of the behavior that you are trying to adopt, and your environment (which we will cover in the next chapter).

In one study conducted by University College London, researchers had ninety-six volunteers choose a healthy drinking, eating, or exercise activity that they wanted to turn into a habit. The study participants were asked to perform their chosen behavior every day in the same context (e.g., during lunch or before dinner) for twelve weeks. The participants chose behaviors like "drinking a bottle of water with lunch," "eating a piece of fruit with lunch," or "running for fifteen minutes before dinner."[25]

During the study, participants were asked to log onto a website each day to report whether they had performed the behavior the previous day and to complete the self-report habit index (SRHI) for the behavior. The SRHI is a self-reported measure of how automatic a behavior has become.

The researchers found that the median time for participants to form their habit was sixty-six days, with a range of eighteen to 254 days. The researchers also found that the group who chose to form an exercise habit took 1.5 times longer to form a habit than the groups who chose to form an eating or drinking habit. More complex habits (like exercising for fifteen minutes) will take longer to form than simpler habits (like eating a piece of fruit).

Manage your expectations accordingly, and be kind to yourself when you are trying to form a new habit. True, long-lasting behavior change usually takes longer than you might like. This is not because you lack self-control or discipline! This is simply the reality of behavior change.

The strategies in this book will help you form stronger habits as quickly and as naturally as possible. My recommendation is to use *the Headlights Method* (see chapter 2) and focus on making one change at a time—what I refer to as your *Stronger Habit of the Month*. With this approach, you identify one behavior each month to stop doing altogether (or to do less often), or you identify one behavior to start doing (or to do more often).

Whenever the behavior that you selected starts to feel automatic, you can then identify your next *Stronger Habit of the Month*. Sometimes it will take longer than thirty days for you to form a new habit, and sometimes you will be able to form a new habit more quickly.

This methodical, science-based approach to self-improvement will be much less painful and much more effective and sustainable than attempting to change too much at once, which is unfortunately what many people try to do. Make one change every month for the next twelve months, and you could transform your life (if you want to) over the next year.

What If You Want to Make More Than One Change Now?

You are certainly allowed to take numerous steps each day to improve how you feel and perform. For example, let's say that the first habit that you want to focus on is to start exercising before every workday. Well, you could certainly also start reducing your consumption of artificial foods at the same time. However, consider any effort beyond your *Stronger Habit of the Month* as a bonus. The positioning here is very important, or you can easily fall into the trap of taking on too much at one time.

It's better to start small and build momentum and confidence, rather than biting off more than you can chew and potentially being overwhelmed after just a few days or weeks. Whenever a behavior starts to feel relatively effortless and automatic (when it becomes a habit), you can then identify the next behavior to focus on. If that happens sooner than a month, then start working on the next change at that time.

CHAPTER SUMMARY

The third level of *The P.O.W.E.R. Pyramid* is the way. Virtually every behavior—good or bad—is part of a process that you can change. This chapter discussed Charles Duhigg's "Habit Loop," along with specific strategies for breaking habits (remove or reduce the cue, swap or shrink the routine, reframe the reward) and for making habits (hook the habit, predict and overcome obstacles, tweak the routine). Here are some questions that you might want to ask yourself as you reflect on this chapter:

- Think of a behavior that you would like to stop doing (or do less often). What are the cue(s) and reward(s) associated with this behavior? How could you use the strategies from this chapter to break this habit?
- Think of a behavior that you would like to start doing (or do more often). How could you use the strategies from this chapter to make this habit stick?
- How often do you think about your future self? Who do you want to become in the future?

CHAPTER 4

ENVIRONMENT

Most of us think we control our own thoughts. Many of our thoughts are primed; they're triggered by our environment.[1]
—Tony Robbins, a #1 *New York Times* best-selling author, entrepreneur, and philanthropist

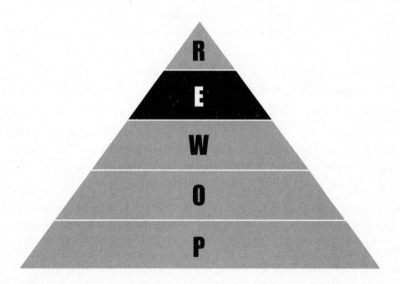

Dr. Brian Wansink is professor and director of the Cornell University Food and Brand Lab, where he is a leading expert in changing eating behavior.[2] In his book *Mindless Eating: Why We Eat More Than We Think*, he talks about one study that he conducted in 1999

on a group of unsuspecting moviegoers who purchased a ticket for a Saturday showing of *Payback*, an action movie starring Mel Gibson.

Each person who bought a ticket was given a free soft drink and a free bucket of popcorn (either a "medium" size or a "large" size). They were told that the theater hoped they would answer a few questions after the movie about the concession stand. The participants were not told they were part of an experiment on eating habits. They were also not told that their popcorn was stale—it had been popped five days earlier.

When the movie ended, each person was asked to complete a brief survey. Each person was also asked to turn in their container of remaining popcorn. All participants had been given a bucket designed to be too big to finish, and each person's bucket was weighed for the remaining contents.

The people who had been given the "large" buckets were told that some other people had been given smaller buckets. They were also told that the average person given a larger bucket tends to eat more than the average person given a smaller bucket. They were then asked if they ate more because they were given a larger container.

Most people were convinced that the size of their bucket would not influence them. However, the data proved otherwise. On average, someone who received a larger bucket ate 53 percent more than someone who received one of the smaller buckets.[3] Remember that this popcorn wasn't any good either. It was so stale that two people actually asked for their money back after the movie. They were reminded that the popcorn had been given to them for free.

As Dr. Wansink writes in *Mindless Eating*, "Everyone—every single one of us—eats how much we eat largely because of what's around us. We overeat not because of hunger but because of family and friends, packages and plates, names and numbers, labels and lights, colors and candles, shapes and smells, distractions and distances, cupboards and containers...Most of us are blissfully unaware of what influences how much we eat."[4]

The fourth level of *The P.O.W.E.R. Pyramid* is **environment**. Your surroundings (physically, digitally, and socially) influence all of your habits, not only your eating habits. In this chapter, you will learn how to change six of your environments, so that you can have more energy, less stress, and higher performance. Let's start in your home…

ENVIRONMENT #1: SLEEP SANCTUARY

Do you feel relaxed when you are in your bedroom? If not, it's time for some changes. Here are four key recommendations:

Beware of Electronics and Lighting

According to the National Sleep Foundation, 95 percent of us use some kind of electronic device within an hour of bedtime on at least a few nights each week.[5] Studies have demonstrated that this reduces sleep quality. In a 2014 experiment led by Dr. Anne-Marie Chang of Penn State University, researchers found that melatonin levels decreased for participants who read on an iPad before bedtime.[6] Melatonin is a hormone that helps induce sleepiness.

In addition, the researchers found that people who read on an iPad before bedtime also took longer to fall asleep, and their sleep quality was lower than those who read physical books in a dimly lit room. Those who read on an iPad before bed also reported being groggier and less alert the next morning, even after getting eight hours of sleep.[7]

The simplest way to improve your sleep quality is to remove any unnecessary clutter, work-related materials, and electronics from your bedroom. If you think you need the sound from a TV to fall asleep, you can swap that routine and turn on a fan or a white noise machine for a more peaceful, light-free source of ambient noise. The National Sleep Foundation also recommends a dark room for sleep.[8] Blackout curtains can be very effective.

Place Your Alarm Clock Carefully

If you use an alarm clock, you could keep it at least ten feet from your bed, so you have to get up to turn it off in the morning. Whether you keep it on the floor or on top of another surface, face it away from you or under something, so that the light and time are not visible. Otherwise, the light from the clock can keep you awake, seeing the time can be stressful if you are struggling to fall asleep, and it can be too easy to snooze in the morning if you only have to roll over to do so.

Optimize Your Bedroom Temperature

The National Sleep Foundation recommends a bedroom temperature between sixty and sixty-seven degrees.[9] You will likely need to sleep under a warm blanket in a room that is this cold. Experiment and determine what works for you though.

Invest in a Quality Mattress and Pillows

You spend about 30 percent of your life in bed. A quality mattress and pillows are some of the best investments that you can make. According to the National Sleep Foundation, most mattresses should be replaced every eight years or so, and pillows should be replaced every couple of years.[10] Whatever sleeping position you prefer, your mattress and pillows should support your spine and help you maintain good posture from head to toe. If your bed sags or you wake up feeling stiff or tired, that could be a sign that it is time for a new bed or pillows.

ENVIRONMENT #2: HEALTHIER HOME KITCHEN

A superior home kitchen setup will lead to better eating habits and make healthy cooking much easier and more enjoyable. *Slim By Design: Mindless Eating Solutions for Everyday Life* is another book written by Dr. Brian Wansink, the expert on changing eating behavior who we discussed at the start of this chapter. In this book, he discusses a study in which he found that the average woman who kept breakfast cereal on her counter weighed twenty-one pounds more than a woman who did not. This same study also found that a woman who kept soda on her counter was twenty-nine pounds heavier, on average, than a woman who did not.[11]

You want healthier foods to be more visible, more accessible, and more convenient. You want unhealthier foods to be less visible, less accessible, and less convenient. Ideally, you would remove all heavily processed items from your kitchen and any other location that you frequent. This removes the visual triggers that initiate many poor eating habits. You can still indulge occasionally, as we will discuss in chapter 6. However, you do not want fattening products to be in sight and within reach at all times. Out of sight, out of body.

If you are not willing to rid your kitchen of junk food (or if you are worried that might lead to a revolt by the people that you live with), you could banish unhealthy items to a less convenient location, like a hallway closet or a mini-fridge in your basement. Another alternative is to "hide" junk foods in your kitchen by keeping them inside of drawers, in foil or dark containers, or in the back of your cabinets, refrigerator, or freezer.

Save the prime real estate in your kitchen for healthier products. You can make nutritious foods more visible by storing them in plastic wrap or clear containers and by placing them in the front of any places where you store foods and drinks. You could also keep some of your healthier items on your counter. One of Dr. Wansink's studies also found that a woman with a fruit bowl on the counter weighed seven pounds less, on average, than one who did not have one.[12]

Healthy Eating Need Not Be Expensive

Many people believe that eating healthy is very costly. However, it does not have to be. You can cut your costs significantly if you purchase items on sale and in bulk (instead of buying products in smaller packages). You can also save money by preparing more of your own meals (instead of dining out). Either way, consider nutritious foods to be an investment in your health, well-being, and performance.

What Are Some Healthy Products to Purchase in Bulk?

In chapter 6, you will learn how to fuel your body and how to read nutrition labels. For now, here is a list of some excellent items to buy and store in bulk in your home kitchen:

- Spices (e.g., chili powder, cinnamon, cumin, oregano, paprika, pepper)
- Eggs (organic and cage-free is best)
- Meat (organic and grass-fed is best; buy in bulk and store in your freezer)
- Fish (organic and wild is best; buy in bulk and store in your freezer)
- Canned fish in water (e.g., tuna or salmon)

- Whole grains (e.g., oats, quinoa, brown rice)
- Vinegars (e.g., apple cider vinegar or balsamic vinegar)
- Extra-virgin olive oil
- Beans and lentils
- Nuts and nut butters
- Fresh/frozen fruits and vegetables

What About Supplements?

You might also want to consider purchasing the following supplements in bulk, based on your dietary needs and the convenience factor. While these items should not replace a proper nutrition program (natural foods are always best), certain supplements can really come in handy, especially during travel:

- Unflavored whey protein powder or vegan protein powder
- Fish oil (supports brain health because it is high in omega-3 fatty acids)
- Multi-vitamin (can fill in some gaps in your nutrition program)
- Greens supplement (can provide essential nutrients if fruits/ vegetables are not accessible)
- Vitamin D (can be obtained from sunlight, but this vitamin is very rare in foods)

Note: Thorne Research and Genuine Health are two supplement companies that are recommended by Precision Nutrition, the world's #1 nutrition coaching and education company.[13]

What Equipment Should You Have in Your Home Kitchen?

Your kitchen should also include essential cooking tools, basic cleaning supplies, and items to serve, store, and transport meals and snacks. You probably have many of these items already. Here is a checklist for essential cooking tools:

- Blender
- Olive oil cooking spray
- Outdoor grill or indoor grill

- Several large spoons and spatulas
- Several sharp knives
- Cutting board
- Measuring cups and spoons
- Pans
- Large pots and/or Crock-Pot
- Baking sheets
- Large mixing bowls
- Oven mitts
- Can opener
- Strainer

Here is a checklist for items for serving, storing, and transporting food and drinks:

- Plates, bowls, silverware, glasses
- Lunch cooler(s) and ice packs
- Tupperware of various sizes
- Water bottles
- Freezer bags
- Snack bags
- Aluminum foil pans
- Aluminum foil

ENVIRONMENT #3: HEALTHIER OFFICE KITCHEN

Many office kitchens look more like a bakery or candy store than a place designed to encourage healthy, high-performing behavior. If you can't resist a treat, you could stay out of the office kitchen. An alternative is to bring and keep healthy, tasty food on hand at work. You could prepare your own meals and snacks in advance. Or you could buy healthy items prepared for you, such as any of the following, many of which are portable and excellent for travel:

- Organic, grass-fed jerky
- Organic, cage-free hard-boiled eggs
- Organic plain, nonfat Greek yogurt

- Nuts or nut butters
- Roasted chickpeas
- Fresh fruit (firmer fruits like apples are best for travel)
- Raw vegetables
- Oats
- Unflavored whey protein powder or vegan protein powder
- Magic Bullet blender (ideal for travel, since it does not take up much space)

Most of these items require no refrigeration, and you can buy them in bulk. Some of them can be eaten on their own, like beef jerky or roasted chickpeas. Others work well together, like Greek yogurt with fresh fruit. If you travel for work, here are two more recommendations:

Bring Food with You

Bringing food with you helps you overcome the obstacle of healthy food not being easily accessible when you travel. Don Monistere, president at TekLinks (a private IT solutions company), is very proactive in this regard. "I have one suitcase that is specifically for non-perishable food, including almonds, peanut butter, protein powder, and sweet potatoes," he told me.

"My colleagues definitely tease me about it, but they aren't laughing in the afternoon when they are hungry," he said. No one is laughing at Don in the gym or at the beach either. Outside of his corporate career, he is a bodybuilding champion in Alabama, and he can do a barbell squat with more than two times his body weight, even though he is in his late forties.

Shop When You Arrive

If you do not want to fill up your luggage in advance, you could purchase healthy items when you arrive at your destination (which Monistere also does for some perishable items). Shopping at your travel location is a strategy used by Elliott Ferguson, president and CEO at Destination D.C., the lead organization to successfully manage and market Washington, D.C. as a premier global convention, tourism, and special events destination.

"When I travel, I make it a habit to stop off at a local drugstore to get packets of tuna, unsalted nuts, and other healthy items," Elliott said. "I'll eat some tuna before I go to a business dinner, so I'm not as hungry, and so I don't make poor eating choices." As discussed in chapter 3, this is an example of how to remove a cue that might otherwise serve as a trigger for an unhealthy habit, like eating junk food at a business event. In this case, the cue is feeling famished.

ENVIRONMENT #4: PAIN-FREE DESK

A stronger office is not only about the food and drinks that surround you. The ergonomics of your workspace make a big difference too. Your desk and computer can significantly increase your chances of experiencing neck or back pain. Here are five key recommendations to reduce and prevent chronic aches:

- **Elevate your laptop.** Laptops encourage you to drop your head to look at your monitor. This puts a lot of strain on your neck. You can create a better setup very easily. Connect your laptop to a separate keyboard, in addition to a separate monitor. Keep your monitor about an arm's length away from you, and elevate it, so that the top half of your monitor is eye level. This will encourage you to keep your head upright, which will reduce the pressure on your neck.
- **Stand up often.** Sitting has come under a lot of fire the last few years, and for good reason. It encourages sedentary behavior and puts 40–90 percent more stress on your lower back than standing, according to Cornell University.[14] You can minimize some of the effects of sitting by standing up and/or walking around for a few minutes every thirty to sixty minutes.
- **Get (or make) an adjustable desk or a standing desk.** More and more companies are providing this benefit. If yours does not, you can create your own by stacking a small table or a

pile of books on top of a standard desk. Over time, you could gradually decrease your time spent seated. Even standing ten to fifteen minutes out of every hour can reduce back pain. You do not need to stand for the entire day.

- **Maintain quality posture.** Whether you sit or stand, be careful not to slouch. Poor posture can erase the benefits of a perfect setup. You will probably feel most comfortable when your arms are at a ninety-degree angle at your elbows (while sitting or standing), and when your legs are at a ninety-degree angle at your knees (while sitting). You might need to raise or lower your chair or desk to achieve such a setup.
- **Create a pain-free desk on the road.** If you will be working out of the office, you could bring a wireless keyboard and a portable monitor stand with you. Doing so would allow you to create a better setup from any remote location.

ENVIRONMENT #5: STRESS-FREE INBOX

One study of nearly 40,000 inboxes found that the average inbox contains more than 8,000 messages.[15] Your inbox can easily become one of your biggest sources of stress and one of the biggest drains of your time and energy. An efficient setup and email management system will reduce anxiety and make you more efficient. Here are three recommendations:

- **Keep your personal email separate.** Forward any non-work emails to your personal email address. Then, delete those messages from your work inbox.
- **Use folders and sub-folders.** File incoming emails by project, client, or some other method. Even if you keep every message that you get (which is not recommended because of the digital clutter that would result), this keeps your main inbox neater and allows you to group relevant messages together. You could also create a "Reference" folder (for storing miscellaneous emails worth keeping) and a "Templates" folder (for storing emails that you plan to send again in the future).

- **Reduce your future clutter.** You can begin by deleting the prior email whenever you get a response to an older message. The newer email obviously contains all the information from the previous one. You can also start unsubscribing from non-essential email lists, and you can be strict about what you sign up to receive through your work email in the future. (You can use your personal email more liberally if you want.) Less incoming email means less future clutter and fewer potential distractions at work.

Like anything, email management can be taken too far. Some people obsess over keeping their inbox at zero all day long. That can become its own source of stress and wasted time and energy. Another approach is to keep your main inbox tidy (not perfect) during the week. If you want, you could try to reach zero at the end of a week or before a vacation.

ENVIRONMENT #6: STRONGER COMMUNITY

Your social environment can impact your behavior even more than your physical environment. If you want to improve your results in life, you might need to cut back on time spent with certain people. You might even need to eliminate some individuals from your life.

Darren Hardy, publisher of *SUCCESS* Magazine, has a thought-provoking philosophy on how to think about the time that you spend with other people. As Hardy writes in *The Compound Effect: Jumpstart Your Income, Your Life, and Your Success*, "There are some people you can spend three hours with, but not three days. Others you can spend three minutes with, but not three hours...Take a look at your relationships and make sure you're not spending three hours with a three-minute person."[16]

In addition to cutting back on time spent with certain people, search for opportunities to build a stronger community around you. Surrounding yourself with healthy, positive people is one of the most effective ways to reinforce your ideal behaviors and take your performance to an even higher level. (Note: In the next chapter, you will learn of four other strategies to reinforce your behavior.) Exercise classes, charity organizations, and business clubs are three kinds of groups where you can look. Even better, you could combine exercise and volunteerism or combine exercise and business.

> **Work Stronger Wisdom**
> "I'm a big believer in the saying that you become the sum of the five people you spend the most time with."
> —Hoby Darling, former CEO at Skullcandy

Combine Exercise and Volunteerism

Service-minded physical activity is a powerful combination for your mind, body, and spirit. My brother, Matt, lives in Manhattan and volunteers with the New York City chapter of Achilles International, a non-profit organization that encourages disabled people to participate in mainstream athletics.[17] Matt serves as a running guide for a blind man named Charles. They wear a belt that connects them at the hip during exercise. Matt provides verbal guidance as they run with other volunteers. These are not leisurely jogs though. They run fast and far. Matt and Charles have completed the New York City Marathon together in under four hours!

In a typical week, I teach a few group exercise classes, and I also volunteer with Back on My Feet (BOMF), a non-profit highlighted in chapter 2. These activities only require three to four hours (combined) of my time each week, and it is impossible to quantify the positive impact that the people in these groups have had on my life.

Combine Exercise and Business

Instead of meeting a co-worker or a client for drinks, a meal, or a meeting inside a conference room, what about going for a walk or a run? This strategy is endorsed by Bob Fleshner, principal at EPICOACH, a career counseling and coaching firm. Previously, Bob served as CEO of the Mid-Atlantic for UnitedHealth Group, a diversified health and well-being company. He told me that he believes that exercise can help you bond with people in a way that is not possible in a typical social or business setting. "When you run with someone, you open up in a way that you otherwise would not," he said. "I think it's partly due to the exercise, but also because you are in motion and not worried about your body language or what the other person is thinking.

"When I took over UnitedHealth for the Mid-Atlantic, one of my areas was Virginia. One day, I got a blistering message from a broker. Our account manager told me the broker just qualified for and ran the Boston Marathon, so I called him back and asked if he wanted to meet me for a run to discuss his problems. We hit it off, and it got to the point where we were running together every other Friday. He eventually became one of our biggest supporters."

In addition to going for a run, you could also combine exercise and business by attending one of the many group fitness classes offered these days. This came up during my conversation with Tara-Nicholle Nelson, founder and chief executive officer at Trans-formational Consumer Insights, a research and management con-sulting firm. She said that "indoor cycling is like golf for female leaders in technology."

"I'll often walk into the room at my local spin studio and I'll know ten to fifteen of the women there," she said. "They are all in big leadership roles. It's a great social environment, and I've also had a lot of business opportunities come out of it."

Start Your Own Exercise Group

You could also get a few friends together and start your own work-out team, like Strauss Zelnick, chairman and CEO at Take-Two In-teractive Software, Inc. a leading developer, publisher, and marketer of interactive entertainment. Strauss has his own exercise group (#TheProgram), which even has its own website. You can check it out at theprogram.nyc. "It happened organically," Strauss told me. "At first, we just had a few guys who were cycling together. Then, we decided to try yoga, and we liked it. Then, we decided to try a high-intensity interval training class at Equinox, and we liked that too.

"Then we started lifting weights together. Other people started coming, and we got onto a schedule where we exercise together at 6:00 a.m. Tuesday through Thursday—and also at 7:00 a.m. on

Fridays when I am in town. People pick and choose what they want to participate in. Training with other people is fun and motivating."

Strauss Zelnick, chairman and CEO at Take-Two Interactive Software

As Chip Heath and Dan Heath write in *Switch: How to Change Things When Change Is Hard*, "Behavior is contagious."[18] This is just as true for good habits as it is for bad habits. The Heath Brothers crystallize this in *Switch* by highlighting a study by Harvard Medical School, in which researchers followed 12,067 people for more than thirty years. They discovered a startling finding: when someone became obese, the odds of that person's close mutual friends becoming obese *increased by 171 percent*, even if the friends lived in different parts of the country.[19] The lead researcher of the study explained this by stating that you form your definition of what is acceptable for yourself by looking at the behavior of the people around you.

LESS CLUTTER = LESS STRESS AND GREATER FOCUS
Studies have analyzed the impact of clutter, and the findings are not positive. Research has demonstrated a link between clutter and unhealthier eating, higher stress, less efficient thinking, and lower overall well-being.[20]

For example, UCLA's Center on Everyday Lives of Families (CELF) has evaluated the impact of clutter in the home. Over a four-year period, they studied thirty-two dual-income, middle-class families living in Los Angeles, California. This labor-intensive project generated almost 20,000 photographs and more than 1,500 hours of videotaped interactions and interviews with the participating families. Among other troubling discoveries, the researchers found that "managing the volume of possessions was such a crushing problem in many homes that it actually elevated levels of stress hormones for mothers."[21]

Other research has looked at the impact of clutter at work. Dr. Sabine Kastner of Princeton University has studied attention for more than twenty years. She has found that visual clutter reduces your brain's performance because clutter makes your brain work harder to filter and focus.[22]

You are probably unaware of how many things that you actually possess (physically and digitally). The longer you have lived or worked in the same place, the more stuff that you have likely accumulated. I once moved to a new apartment after living in my prior residence for about a decade. As I prepared for my move, I was stunned to discover how many useless items I had managed to jam into closets, drawers, and cabinets. The most noteworthy item was in the back of one of my cabinets: it was a box of rice that had expired more than six years earlier!

There are a few different ways to tackle your existing clutter. One approach is to block out a few hours (or more) to make a big dent at one time. Another approach is to set aside ten to fifteen minutes (or some other amount of time) each day for getting organized. Some combination of these two approaches is probably best, so do what works for you.

Organizing and de-cluttering your various environments (at work and at home) is one of the top ways to reduce your stress and increase your focus. You can start by trashing, selling, or donating items that you have not used in the last year (other than items that hold sentimental value). As French writer Antoine de Saint-Exupéry once said, "Perfection is achieved, not when there is nothing more to add, but when there is nothing left to take away."

CHAPTER SUMMARY

The fourth level of *The P.O.W.E.R. Pyramid* is environment. Your surroundings (physically, digitally, and socially) influence all of your behavior. This chapter highlighted tips on how to de-clutter and enhance six of your environments:

- Environment #1: Sleep sanctuary
- Environment #2: Healthier home kitchen
- Environment #3: Healthier office kitchen
- Environment #4: Pain-free desk
- Environment #5: Stress-free inbox
- Environment #6: Stronger community

Here are some questions that you might want to ask yourself as you reflect on this chapter:

- How could you turn your bedroom into a more peaceful sleeping environment?
- How could you create a healthier eating environment around you?
- How could you build a stronger community around you? Which groups and organizations could you get involved with to meet like-minded people?

CHAPTER 5

REINFORCEMENT

*Discipline—strict order, regimen, and control—might appear
to be the opposite of total freedom—the power to act, speak,
or think without any restrictions. But, in fact, discipline is the
pathway to freedom.*
　　　—Jocko Willink and Leif Babin in *Extreme Ownership:
How U.S. Navy Seals Lead and Win*[1]

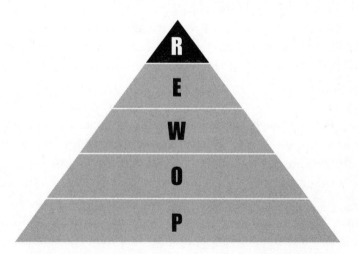

Imagine if there were no laws for driving. In such a world, all of us
would be able to drive in any lane, go as fast as we wanted, and race
through intersections when we did not feel like stopping. Think of
the pandemonium that would result. Think of how much better off
you are because of the various laws that we all follow on the road.

Unfortunately, a world with no driving laws is a good metaphor for the lack of boundaries that exist around many of our habits in today's society. Drive-through restaurants and convenience stores provide us with twenty-four/seven access to artificial "foods" that our bodies are not built to consume. Smartphones and laptops allow us to work twenty-four/seven and from virtually anywhere in the world. Technology also allows us to be entertained for hours without moving.

You can either allow yourself to be controlled by our turbulent world, or you can take control of your behavior by bringing more order to life. You do not need to live like a robot. However, a reasonable amount of structure helps you form stronger habits more easily and makes change much easier.

Structure prevents chaos. The fifth level of *The P.O.W.E.R. Pyramid* is **reinforcement**. In this chapter, you will learn four powerful strategies to reinforce your ideal behavior and hold yourself accountable.

STRATEGY #1: TRACK YOURSELF

When my brother Matt and I were teenagers, we had part-time jobs as caddies at a local country club in our hometown. On days that we worked, we arrived at the golf course around 6:00 a.m., and we waited to be assigned to our golfers for the day. Then, we walked the eighteen-hole course for about four hours. During each round, we carried a golf bag on each shoulder (about fifty pounds of weight in total).

I hated this job and worked inconsistently for two summers. (We did not have a fixed schedule, so we could show up as much or as little as we wanted.) Matt, on the other hand, worked religiously during summers and holiday breaks for nearly a decade. One summer, he even caddied on thirty-nine straight days, en route to earning more than $13,000 in cash in less than four months. How many teenagers make that kind of money legally?

There is a key reason why Matt and I had such different experiences. He set financial goals for himself and tracked his progress toward those goals. Whenever he got home from work, he updated a spreadsheet that he had created to monitor his earnings. Each day, he could see and feel his progress. In comparison, I did not have any financial goals or a system to measure my progress/earnings. As a result, the job felt like pointless torture to me.

The strategy of tracking came up repeatedly during my interviews for this book. Dr. Larry Senn, chairman at Senn-Delaney, and Don Monistere, president at TekLinks, each told me that they use fitness trackers to monitor sleep duration and quality. Michelle Kluz, founder of The Barre Project and Urban Savage (an activewear line), told me that she has used MyFitnessPal to track virtually everything she has eaten for the last couple of years. Kent Wuthrich, a marketing and product design/development consultant and small business owner, told me that he writes down everything he will eat for the day when he wakes up. Juan Uro, executive vice president at the NBA, told me that he has been tracking pace and distance for all of his runs for over fifteen years. "You cannot measure progress unless you track it," he said. "Accountability can be as simple as winning against your own targets."

> **Work Stronger Wisdom**
> "Numbers and analytics can be very motivating to a lot of people."
> —Robin Thurston, CEO at Helix (a consumer
> genomics company) and co-founder of
> MapMyFitness (acquired by Under
> Armour in 2013)

Track Your Progress

Research has demonstrated the effectiveness of monitoring your progress. For example, one meta-analysis (led by Dr. Benjamin Harkin of the University of Sheffield) looked at 138 studies that were focused mainly on personal health goals. The researchers found that the more frequent the monitoring, the higher the chances of success. They also found that recording progress physically or reporting progress publicly led to even greater results.[2]

Other research has led to additional insights on how to maximize the impact of tracking. According to a concept known as "small-area hypothesis," motivation increases when you focus your attention on whatever is smaller in size between (a) how far you have come and (b) how far you have to go. In other words, when you are getting started, you are better off tracking *accumulated progress* and focusing on what you have achieved so far (not how far you have to go, which will be de-motivating). When you are at least half-way to a goal, you are better off tracking *remaining progress* and focusing on how close you are to your target.[3]

Track Your Habits
In addition to (or instead of) tracking your progress, you can also track your habits. Doing so forces you to determine and quantify specific behaviors that will get you where you want to be. You can track your behavior daily (which is ideal) or weekly. If you find at the end of a month that you are not getting the results that you desire, that could be evidence to identify new behaviors to focus on and track for the following month.

Track a Streak
You can also start and track a streak. Cal Ripken, Jr. holds a Major League Baseball record for playing in 2,632 consecutive games between 1982 and 1998. It is hard to imagine that he would never have missed a game without everyone monitoring how many he had played in a row. Think of the psychology involved here. As your streak gets longer, you build more and more momentum, and the price for stopping also gets larger and larger.

You could start a streak to see how many days you can do or avoid any behavior, or you could give yourself advance permission to decide after thirty days (or some other amount of time) if you want to keep going. A streak does not need to occur every day. Ripken's applied only to games. Yours could be for one day each week, or for all weekdays, for all weekend days, or for all workdays.

While there a number of ways you can track yourself, what is most important is that you track something. As Darren Hardy, publisher of *SUCCESS* Magazine, writes in *The Compound Effect*, "All winners are trackers."[4]

STRATEGY #2: WORK WITH A CREDIBLE COACH

When Amy Cozad Magaña walked on to her college diving team in 2009 at the University of Indiana, she initially felt like a "nobody" (her word). Most of the girls on the team were there on scholarships. However, her mindset shifted quickly due to the support and guidance provided by her legendary diving coach, Dr. Jeff Huber. "One day, he called me into his office and told me I had the potential to become an Olympian if I followed his advice," Amy told me. "Initially, I thought to myself, 'Are you kidding me?' but I kept my head down and worked very hard."

Amy went on to become a US national champion in synchronized 10-meter platform diving. The vision that Dr. Huber established for her also became a reality. She qualified for the 2016 Olympics and represented the United States in Rio de Janeiro.

A *Credible Coach* will help you tap into inner potential that you might not see or be able to fully unleash on your own. The best athletes in the world all rely on coaches. Why not follow their lead and hire someone to help you maximize your health, well-being, and performance?

Many successful businesspeople rely on coaches to feel and perform their best. For example, Elliott Ferguson, president and CEO at Destination D.C, told me that he usually works out one-on-one with a trainer once or twice a week. He also takes group exercise classes led by trainers. "No matter how long you have been working out or how great you think your regimen is, you need an expert who can help you maximize your results," he said.

You could work with a coach in-person, via phone, or online. This last option works well for Rhonda Vetere, chief technology officer at Estée Lauder Companies. Rhonda travels over 75 percent of the time. She is an endurance athlete and told me that she has been working with a coach remotely since January 2016. "I tell him all of my races for the year, and all of my travel for the next four to five months, although it will obviously change," she said. "He designs my training calendar. We use an app called TrainingPeaks where he uploads my workouts. I look at the program one week at a time, and then open the app daily to see what I need to do. After each workout,

Elliott Ferguson, president and CEO at Destination D.C.

I record what I have done." (Notice how Rhonda utilizes coaching *and* tracking.)

Work Stronger Wisdom

"I have had a coach for many periods over the last couple of decades. It's not that I don't know how to coach myself at this point. It just saves me time and effort. A coach can facilitate reaching your goals and help hold you accountable."

—Frank Karbe, an executive recognized in 2005
and 2013 by CEO Challenges as
"World's Fittest CEO"

Select the Right Coach for You

You will probably have to evaluate a number of coaches to find one or several who are right for you. Coaches have vastly different styles, personalities, and areas of expertise. Look for people who have experience working with individuals like you, and look for people who truly bring out the best in you.

Your coach could help you manage your overall performance, or your coach could help you in a specific area. Bob Fleshner, principal at EPICOACH, told me that he got private coaching in yoga, and it made a huge difference for him. "I took group yoga classes several years ago with my wife, and I absolutely hated it," said Bob. "But, more recently, I got individualized yoga lessons, and it completely changed everything for me. Now, I do yoga by myself every other day for forty minutes a day."

Hold Up Your Side of the Relationship

You also need to be coachable. While another person can help you stay on track, you cannot outsource your motivation to anyone else. Motivation must come from within. Even if you hire a private coach, you will still be on your own for over 95 percent of each week. As the late motivational speaker, Jim Rohn, once said, "You can't hire someone else to do your push-ups for you."

If private coaching is not feasible, group coaching is a cheaper alternative that can be very effective as well. As discussed in chapter 4, group classes can also be a great way to meet like-minded individuals who are interested in health, well-being, and performance.

STRATEGY #3: CLIMB MEANINGFUL MOUNTAINS

In the spring of 2009, a cardiologist informed Chris Tsakalakis (a technology executive and former president at StubHub, the world's largest ticket marketplace) that he would need open-heart surgery to repair a genetic issue. Chris was only forty-one years old at the time. "My initial thought when I heard that news was that I didn't want my sons to grow up without a dad," Chris told me.

Tsakalakis had the surgery four months later. When he first arrived home ten days after that, he could only walk around the block, about a half mile. He initially needed to lay down and recover after each lap. After being home for two months, Chris went back to work part-time and started cardiac rehab at a local hospital. He used the distance between these locations as a way to rebuild his strength. He would park at the hospital and walk over two miles to his office, where he would shower and get to work. After work, he would walk over two miles back.

While in the hospital after his surgery, Chris had decided that he would run the Chicago Marathon with his wife the following year. He joined the Leukemia & Lymphoma Society's Team in Training program. One of Chris's best friends had recently died of leukemia, and Chris decided to raise money in his friend's honor for leukemia research.

In October 2010 (the year after his surgery), Chris and his wife did the Chicago Marathon together. It took them over five and a half hours to finish, and Chris had to walk at the end, but they completed all 26.2 miles.

Chris Tsakalakis and his wife after completing the Chicago Marathon
(the year after Chris had open-heart surgery)

Every year, thousands of people of all ages, backgrounds, and fitness levels climb what I refer to as a *Meaningful Mountain*. This is a voluntary physical challenge that takes you out of your comfort zone and builds greater fitness, discipline, confidence, and mental tough-ness in the process. Whether you are a person recovering after major surgery, someone who wants to adopt a more active lifestyle, or an elite athlete who wants to reach even higher, these experiences make you stronger and reinforce your purpose and motivation to take care of yourself. "Signing up for races gives me something to work to-ward," said Michelle Kluz, a competitive runner and founder of The Barre Project and Urban Savage. "They really keep you on track."

Meaningful Mountains can also help you create lifelong memories with people that you care about. Many people complete challenges with friends and family. However, if your friends or family are unable or uninterested in climbing the mountain that you have in mind, they can still come and cheer you on during your event. My family came and supported me when I competed in the Obstacle Course Racing (OCR) World Championships in Canada (the year before finishing this book). The event was so much more meaningful to me because of the time that we spent together the day of the event and the day be-fore and after. Any adventure—especially a challenging one—is more meaningful when it is experienced with people who matter to you.

Michelle Kluz, founder of The Barre Project and Urban Savage

Work Stronger Wisdom
"Every year, I pick something I call a 'crucible event,' an idea I got from a friend of mine who is an old Navy SEAL commander. The idea is to pick something that's gonna push me beyond what I can do right now, something scary that I'm really gonna have to train for. I tailor my training program around whatever my crucible event is for the year."

—Hoby Darling, former CEO at Skullcandy

Hoby Darling, former CEO at Skullcandy

Which Mountain Should You Climb?

Identify a challenge that you are 50–75 percent confident that you can achieve with your best effort and focus. Why 50–75 percent? Feeling 75–100 percent confident is a sign that it's probably not bold enough for you and that achieving it would probably not be very meaningful for you. Feeling less than 50 percent confident is a sign that it's probably too bold for you to pursue at this point.

There are many options for which mountains you could climb. There are challenges for all ages, for all fitness levels, and for every distance imaginable, ranging from 100-meter sprint races to ultra-marathons and century bike rides that are over one hundred miles long. There are powerlifting competitions and bodybuilding/physique contests (for men and women). There are popular endurance events, like 5K runs, marathons, and triathlons. There are also less well-known endurance events, like stand-up paddleboard races, a personal favorite for Wyatt Everhart, an Emmy Award–winning meteorologist who I interviewed for this book. There are also obstacle races of various themes, distances, and difficulty.

Work Stronger Wisdom

"I'm more successful at work when I'm racing than when I'm not racing."

—Ken Lubin, managing director at ZRG Partners (a boutique executive recruiting firm) and founder of Executive Athletes, an online community of thousands of executives who are passionate about sports and high performance

Ken Lubin, founder of Executive Athletes

Instead of participating in an organized event, you could also tackle your own physical challenge (e.g., a thirty day challenge), or you could try to set a new "PR" (personal record) for a specific exercise or activity. For example, this is a strategy used by small business owner Kent Wuthrich. "Every three to six months, I choose a new physical goal that I want to achieve," he told me. "Right now, I want to put on some size.

"After this, I will choose a new goal. Maybe I will try to get super lean. Maybe I will try to build up to squatting a certain amount, or to running a mile in a certain time. I still do some full-body workouts all year long, but these specific challenges allow me to be able to accomplish things that make me say, 'Wow, look at what I achieved.'"

If you really want to take this strategy literally, you could even climb a *real* mountain. In addition to running marathons with his wife, Mukesh Aghi, president at the U.S.-India Strategic Partnership Forum (USISPF), has climbed some of the highest, deadliest peaks in the world. Mukesh told me about his first attempt to climb Mont Blanc, which is both the tallest mountain in Europe and the one with the highest fatality rate.

During Mukesh's first try, the weather changed abruptly when his group was three-fourths of the way up. A ferocious blizzard started, and temperatures plunged to twenty degrees below zero. The goal then shifted from trying to conquer the mountain to trying to survive. "The storm lasted almost twelve hours," he told me. "We decided we could not climb any higher and had to go back down, but everything was white and soft, so we could not tell where the crevasses were. We had to go slowly, inch by inch, to make our way down safely. The lesson was that it is okay to retreat, just like in business. You have to be able to adapt and come back another day."

When I asked Mukesh if he came back to Mont Blanc another day, he told me there was "nothing interesting" about his second attempt to reach the summit. They just made it to the top and back down safely that time.

Meaningful Mountains will challenge you, and that is what makes them so rewarding. As psychologist Mihaly Csikszentmihalyi writes in his book *Flow: The Psychology of Optimal Experience*, "The best moments usually occur when a person's body or mind is stretched to its limits in a voluntary effort to accomplish something difficult and worthwhile. Optimal experience is thus something that we *make* happen...Such experiences are not necessarily pleasant at the time they occur."[5]

You could climb a *Meaningful Mountain* near your home, or you could travel to a new city or foreign country and turn your challenge into an even bigger adventure. Whatever you decide, get out of your comfort zone, and include your co-workers, friends, and family, either as fellow participants or as cheerleaders. Once you climb your mountain, celebrate your achievement. Then, start looking for the next one. Never stop climbing.

Me at a Tough Mudder obstacle course race

STRATEGY #4: ESTABLISH PERSONAL POLICIES

While some people see themselves as "free spirits" or "rebels" who don't like too much structure, the reality is that each of us follows many rules, no matter how free-spirited or rebellious you think you are. Whether you call them rules, policies, laws, guidelines, standards, codes of conduct, boundaries, principles, philosophies, or something else, you follow them and they make your life better. They keep you on track, they reinforce positive behaviors, and they prevent chaos in your life. They also prevent you from wasting time and energy deciding how to deal with inevitable short-term temptations.

In addition to the driving laws highlighted at the start of this chapter, you also follow certain policies at work, including what you can wear and what you cannot wear. You follow certain policies at stores, including waiting on lines and not cutting people in front of you. You follow certain policies with your bills, including paying certain fees by certain dates.

Many high performers also implement what I refer to as *Personal Policies*, which are self-imposed guidelines designed to reinforce your long-term interests. For example, Sam Shank, CEO and co-founder at HotelTonight (the world's leading hotel booking app), found that drinking coffee later in the day resulted in him staying up too late. So, he established a policy for himself, in which he does not drink caffeine after 12:00 p.m.[6]

Chip Bergh, president and CEO at Levi Strauss & Co., found that his family (him, his wife, and their eight-year-old daughter) was more focused on technology than each other during shared meals. So, his family established a policy in which they do not keep their devices at the table when they are eating together.

Robin Thurston, CEO at Helix, found that he was using his phone to spend too much time on LinkedIn, Twitter, and Facebook. So, he instituted a policy in which he can only visit those websites from his laptop. In order to make this policy easy to follow, he deleted the apps off his phone. This is an excellent example of engineering your environment in a way that supports your desired behavior.

In today's world, we are surrounded twenty-four/seven by harmful or low-value temptations that can keep you from being your best. Your body, your career, and your life will pay the price if you give in every, or most, times that you are presented with something that provides immediate gratification. Why not establish some *Personal Policies* for yourself? What feels reasonable for one person could feel too strict or not regimented enough for someone else, so you have to determine what works for you.

The Ultimate Personal Policy: Honor Every Commitment

Some people only keep their commitments when it is convenient. I used to be that way in my twenties. One day, my girlfriend at the time told me that she didn't feel like she could trust me because of how often I was late or forgetful. Her comment really got my attention. It was a major turning point for me. These days, I am absolutely maniacal about keeping promises made to myself and to other people. I cannot tell you how often this approach reinforces commitments that I might have bailed on earlier in my life.

We all recognize the personal and professional consequences of not following through on "major" commitments. However, *every* broken commitment erodes the trust that you have in yourself and the trust that other people have in you. When it comes to keeping promises made to yourself and to others, perfection (a word not to be used lightly) must be the goal. If you break a commitment, there better be a damn good reason.

Of course, there are exceptions. If you commit to a workout, but your child gets sick and needs to go to the hospital, you would obviously put your child's well-being over your exercise session. What you should not do, however, is blow off a scheduled workout (or any other commitment) if you are simply not in the mood to follow through when the time comes.

If you are wondering how you can keep every promise that you make, it is simple. Do not commit in the first place unless you are willing and able to do whatever it takes to make it happen. Before you make any commitment, ask yourself, "Am I one hundred percent certain that I am willing and capable of honoring this?" The answer to that question will often be "no" or "I am not sure yet." That's completely fine. Many times, "yes" is the wrong answer, even though that might be hard to admit to yourself or uncomfortable to say to someone else.

When you do decide the answer is "yes" though, let that be the end of it. There should not be any debate or bail-outs when the time comes to follow through. It does not matter whether you get really busy or are not in the mood. When your commitment is to another person, it also does not matter whether that person is homeless or a billionaire. Once you make a promise, keep it. Will this approach be difficult? Absolutely. Will this approach be worth it? Absolutely.

Without this *Personal Policy*, how do you know when it is okay to break a promise and when it is not? How can you build trust with other people and with yourself? Is it not simpler, and in your best interest, to decide that you will honor every commitment that you make, no matter how big, how small, or to whom?

When you honor every commitment, you will not waste any time or energy deciding what counts and what does not; you will never have to deal with the inevitable guilt from breaking a promise; and the trust that you have in yourself, and that others have in you, will grow exponentially. You can make excuses, or you can get results. You cannot do both. Honor every commitment that you make. Every. Single. One.

Work Stronger Wisdom

"My biggest priorities are my family and friends; my work; fitness; and charitable work and mentoring. That means many things I'd like to do don't make the list. You have to own your choices. It's not that you're too busy to take care of yourself. You just make other choices."

—Strauss Zelnick, chairman and CEO of Take-Two Interactive Software Inc.

CHAPTER SUMMARY

The fifth level of *The P.O.W.E.R. Pyramid* is reinforcement. Structure prevents chaos. This chapter highlighted four strategies that you can use to reinforce your ideal behavior and hold yourself accountable:

- Strategy #1: Track yourself
- Strategy #2: Work with a *Credible Coach*
- Strategy #3: Climb *Meaningful Mountains*
- Strategy #4: Establish *Personal Policies*

Here are some questions that you might want to ask yourself as you reflect on this chapter:

- Have certain strategies been more effective for you than others in terms of holding yourself accountable in the past? How can you use these strategies in the future?
- Have you had success in the past by tracking yourself in a certain way? How can you follow a similar approach in the future?
- How often do you honor the commitments that you make to yourself and to other people? Are there certain people or certain areas where it is time to start keeping more of your promises?

When you combine a stronger mindset (purpose and optimism), strategies for changing your behavior (the way), surroundings that support your desired behavior (environment), and strategies to hold yourself accountable (reinforcement), you will have the P.O.W.E.R to accomplish anything. Next, we will discuss *The Stronger Cycle*, and you will learn *what* to change in order to increase your energy, decrease your stress, and maximize your performance.

Part II

THE STRONGER CYCLE

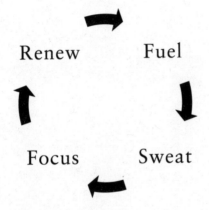

Renew   Fuel

Focus   Sweat

Chapter 6

FUEL

Every bite you take is either fighting disease or feeding it.
—Nutrition expert Heather Morgan, MS, NLC

"My wife and I are trying this new diet," said my colleague Ron. "What's that?" I asked.

"It's an all-liquid, all-fruit diet. You just drink a fruit smoothie three times a day. You can apparently lose ten pounds in two weeks and you don't have to exercise," he said.

Fast forward to the next day, and I see Ron drinking a soda and eating some pizza in the office kitchen. I did not say anything, but he looked at me sheepishly and said, "I forgot to bring my smoothies to work today, so I'm gonna get back on my diet again tomorrow."

The next day, we ran into each other again at lunch. This time, he was eating a TV dinner that he had just taken out of the microwave. "Yeah, that diet didn't work for me," he said. "I couldn't take it. It was too hard to drink every meal."

There are many myths about nutrition. Here are three of the most common:

- Myth #1: You need to follow a trendy, rigid, or complicated diet.
- Myth #2: You need to force yourself to eat foods that you dislike.
- Myth #3: If it sounds healthy, it is healthy.

In this chapter, we'll address each of these misconceptions. You will also learn six key eating habits that will make you healthier, give you more energy, and increase your brainpower. The first three habits are the key behaviors to adopt. The last three habits make the first three habits easier to follow. Let's tackle the top two nutrition myths first.

WHY FAD DIETS DON'T WORK

If you want to feel better and perform better, you do not need to overhaul your nutrition plan all at once. You can dramatically improve your energy, body composition, and brainpower by adopting new eating habits one at a time. As we discussed in the introduction of this book, small habits—bad or good—add up quickly.

Fad diets do not work for many reasons. First of all, they are too restrictive and abrupt. Instead of a gradual approach, they force you to make major changes immediately. Secondly, they set you up to fail. When you go on a diet, you are basically telling yourself, "This is temporary. I only need to eat like this for a period of time, and then I can go back to eating what I *really* want to eat." There is no real, long-term commitment to change your behavior.

Some people do lose weight initially by dieting. However, rapid weight loss usually comes from dehydration and lost muscle, not from large reductions in body fat. In addition, the faster you lose weight, the more likely you will gain it right back. In fact, research by Dr. Traci Mann of UCLA has found that more than 40 percent of people starting a diet will actually *gain* weight.[1]

Focus on habits, not diets. Different nutritional plans can be effective, as long as you primarily consume real foods with natural ingredients. A habit-based approach is a key recommendation by Precision Nutrition (PN), the world's #1 nutrition coaching and education company. I'm a certified coach through PN, and they are *the* resource that I recommend on all things nutrition. They have worked with thousands of average men and women, in addition to Olympians, professional athletes, and professional sports teams in the NFL, NHL, and NBA.[2]

As PN's co-founder, Dr. John Berardi, writes, "We prefer a nutritional progression model (which builds habits intelligently and sustainably over time) versus asking people to 'follow a diet' (which means doing a full lifestyle overhaul on Day One)."[3]

NUTRITIOUS AND DELICIOUS

I used to have a roommate named Todd. One day, Todd told me that he wanted to get healthier. The following Sunday night, he bought some celery sticks at the supermarket. He placed them in our refrigerator when he got home. His plan was to snack on the sticks throughout the week. On Friday, he threw the unopened bag in the garbage.

Many people, like Todd, have an all-or-nothing philosophy when it comes to nutrition. With this mindset, foods can either be nutritious but unpleasant (like raw vegetables), or unhealthy but delicious (like pizza). In reality, there are four kinds of fuel, as depicted in a 2x2 matrix that I refer to as *The Fuel Quadrant*.

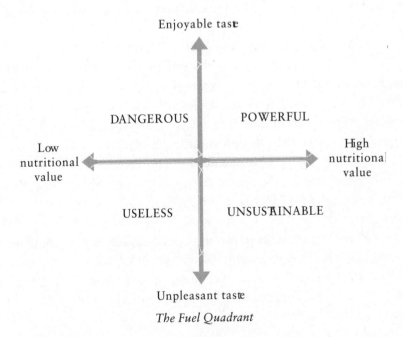

The Fuel Quadrant

"Useless" foods are unpleasant and provide little or no nutritional value. Doritos fall into this category for me, since they provide few nutrients, and they taste terrible to me. If you like Doritos, however, they would be a "dangerous" food for you. "Dangerous" foods are enjoyable but provide little or no value. Ice cream falls into the "dangerous" category for me.

"Unsustainable" foods provide a lot of nutritional value, but are unpleasant. Celery fell into this category for Todd. Sardines fall into this category for me. While loaded with nutrients, they gross me out. "Powerful" foods pack a strong nutritional punch *and* taste great. Oven-roasted vegetables fall into this category for me.

The less you like the foods that you eat (or the workouts that you do), the less likely you will stick with them over the long term. You do not need to torture yourself with "unsustainable" foods. You can replace them with other nutrient-dense items (e.g., getting omega-3 fatty acids from fish oil or wild salmon instead of sardines) or you can turn them into "powerful" foods by adding healthy, natural flavor to improve the taste. You do not need to deprive yourself completely of "dangerous" foods either. You can absolutely enjoy occasional unhealthy indulgences, as long as the bulk of your calories come from natural, nutrient-dense products. (More to come on that later in this chapter.)

How Can You Make Healthy Foods Taste Better?

There are many ways to naturally enhance the taste of a healthy food that might otherwise be unappetizing. For example, you could add olive oil, vinegar, juice from a lemon or lime, fresh fruit, a spice or herb, some onion or garlic, or a natural salsa. Include one extra at a time, and err on the side of less rather than more.

For example, if raw vegetables are an "unsustainable" food for you (like they are for me), there are many ways that you could make them more palatable. Here are three ideas:

- *Sautée with natural flavor.* Cook vegetables in a pot or pan with a tablespoon of olive oil and natural flavor like garlic, chopped onion, or a spice (e.g., cumin). This works well for green leafy vegetables like spinach or kale.

- *Season and roast.* Chop and toss vegetables with olive oil, salt, and pepper, and then roast them in the oven. This works well for firmer vegetables, like broccoli, asparagus, cauliflower, peppers, carrots, sweet potatoes, and squash.
- *Hide.* Rather than eating vegetables on the side, you could also hide them in a stew or in a fruit smoothie. Broccoli, cauliflower, peppers, carrots, and tomatoes work well in stews. Spinach and kale (raw or frozen) work well in smoothies.

A step-by-step process on creating nutritious, delicious meals is provided at the end of this chapter.

STRONGER EATING HABIT #1: WAKE UP, FUEL UP

The fuel (or lack of fuel) that you consume in the morning sets the tone for your eating habits, your energy, and your performance later that day. Skipping breakfast can make you more lethargic and make you more likely to over-eat when you finally break your fast.

Unlike a typical low-value breakfast (e.g., a bagel with cream cheese or juice with cereal), the best breakfasts provide a nutrient-dense balance of quality protein, vegetables, healthy fats, and fibrous carbs. You also want to drink at least sixteen to twenty-four ounces of water when you wake up.

> **Work Stronger Wisdom**
> "If I work out and eat a healthy breakfast in the morning, I'm probably going to have a good eating day. I find that I don't get as tempted to eat junk food when I start the day in a good way."
> —Jennifer Carr-Smith, senior vice president and general manager, North America Local at Groupon, an e-commerce marketplace

While certain foods and meals are typically associated with certain times of day, this is arbitrary. There's no real reason why you could not eat eggs for dinner or beans for breakfast—if you enjoy eating eggs and if you enjoy eating beans. Here are two examples of more traditional breakfasts:

- *Breakfast smoothie.* This is a great option when you are short on time. Your protein source could be protein powder (such as unflavored whey protein powder or a vegan option), organic, plain, nonfat Greek yogurt, or pasteurized egg whites (which are safe to consume without cooking). You could add raw/frozen spinach or kale for your vegetables. You could add fresh/frozen berries for your fibrous carbs. You could add nut butter for healthy fat.
- *Vegetable omelet plus oatmeal.* This is a great option for a hot meal that you can prepare in less than fifteen minutes. The eggs provide your primary source of protein and can include vegetables like peppers, broccoli, or spinach. The oats serve as your fibrous carbs. You could add healthy fat to your oats by including chopped nuts. You could spice up this meal by adding cinnamon and fresh fruit to your oatmeal, or by adding a natural salsa to your omelet.

Wake up, fuel up is easy to hook into your schedule since waking up serves as the cue to do the habit. As discussed in chapter 3, there are two main obstacles to forming this routine. First of all, you need to have the ingredients and relevant cooking tools in your home. Secondly, you have to make time in the morning to prepare and eat the meal. You can overcome these obstacles by getting up a bit earlier, and by purchasing ingredients in advance. If you want to save even more time in the morning, you could prepare part or all of your breakfast the night or weekend before (more to come on that later in this chapter).

Should You Fuel Up Before a Morning Workout?

This is ultimately a personal preference, so experiment and find out what works best for you. If you work out first thing in the morning, you might prefer to fuel up before and after (my preference), or you might prefer to exercise on an empty stomach and only fuel up afterwards. If you choose the former and time is limited, a smaller and/or liquid meal before your workout is a good option.

STRONGER EATING HABIT #2: RE-FUEL EVERY THREE TO FOUR HOURS

In each episode of *Dual Survival* on the Discovery Channel, a pair of survival experts is dropped into one of the world's harshest, most extreme environments.[4] They are then tasked with finding their way out, despite having very limited resources. Regardless of the location or climate, one of the biggest challenges that the survival experts face is making fire. After they manage to get one started, the next challenge is to keep the fire going. Their approach is to gradually add fuel to the fire to keep it burning.

While this is not exactly what happens inside your body, this is a way to think about your metabolism and how to fuel yourself. Think of habit #1 (wake up, fuel up) as a way to start your fire. Think of habit #2 (re-fuel every three to four hours) as a way to keep your fire going. Re-fueling throughout the day with smaller, more frequent meals and snacks will give your body and brain a steady supply of energy and nutrients. Larger, less frequent meals provide inconsistent energy, and they can make you feel stuffed and bloated.

Another benefit of re-fueling every three to four hours is that you will never get famished. This habit therefore also serves as a way to remove/reduce a cue that often leads to poor nutritional choices. Starving yourself in an attempt to cut back on calories can backfire and lead to over-eating.

Ideally, you want to develop a fairly consistent schedule when you eat at similar times on most days. By eating every three to four hours, you will eat four to five times each day. In this case, three of your fuel/re-fuel sessions would be meals. You would also have one or two small snacks each day (e.g., in the mid-morning between breakfast and lunch and another one in the afternoon between lunch and dinner).

The amount of calories to consume in each meal or snack depends on a variety of factors, including your body type and goals, your activity level, and how often you eat. In general, opt for light snacks that contain at least ten grams of protein and a few grams of fiber. Here are three examples:

- Organic plain, nonfat Greek yogurt with fresh berries
- Nuts or nut butter
- Roasted chickpeas

Remember to follow *the Headlights Method*. The eventual goal is to get to the point where you are re-fueling every three to four hours with natural, nutrient dense meals and snacks. Take it one meal or snack at a time though. Focus on breakfast first. After you have formed that habit, you could then work on having one more healthy meal (or snack) each day. Once that has become pretty automatic for you, you could then work on having a third nutrient-dense meal (or snack) each day, and so on.

What about Intermittent Fasting?

All of us do some form of fasting every day. Unless you wake up and eat throughout the night, you already fast for at least ten to twelve consecutive hours on a daily basis (the time between your last meal of the day and your first meal the next day).

Advocates of Intermittent Fasting (IF) recommend that you increase the duration of your fasting intervals. Some IF approaches recommend a consistent schedule (e.g., fast for sixteen hours, eat during the next eight hours, repeat), while other IF approaches recommend just doing one or two longer fasts each week.[5] Clearly, IF differs from the recommendations in this chapter, so let's address it directly.

Some research has indicated that IF, when implemented carefully, may provide benefits for health and longevity. However, IF should not be viewed as a "magic bullet" that can be used to compensate for binges or poor food choices. As Dr. John Berardi of Precision Nutrition writes, "Randomly skipping meals while continuing to eat a diet high in processed foods won't help you lose fat or improve your health."[6]

Intermittent Fasting is not required for maximizing your energy or performance. It's also not where you should start if you have subpar eating habits, if you do not sleep well, or if you are under a lot of stress. According to Dr. Berardi, such a person "really shouldn't bother with intermittent fasting at all."[7]

If you would like to learn more about Intermittent Fasting, I recommend that you read Precision Nutrition's report on the subject. You can download their report at https://www.precisionnutrition.com/intermittent-fasting.

STRONGER EATING HABIT #3: DRINK WATER, NOT CALORIES OR CHEMICALS

You are what you eat *and drink*. Water makes up about 60 percent of your body weight. You need a lot of it to feel and perform your best and to support a number of essential functions. Dehydration can lead to cramping, nausea, headaches, fatigue, irritability, weaker athletic performance, and reduced mental capacity.

You can drink more water by hooking it onto meals, snacks, and breaks. If you are looking for an easy, natural, delicious way to spice it up, you could create your own infused water. Test out different combinations using herbs like mint, spices like cinnamon, vegetables like cucumbers, and fruits like lemons, limes, or berries.

Various factors influence how much water you need. This includes your size (larger people generally need to drink more), the climate (warmer environments generally lead to higher water requirements), and your activity level (those who are more active typically need to drink more). You also need to drink more water (and avoid alcohol, since it will dehydrate you) when you fly due to the dry air and low humidity found in a typical aircraft.

Depending on your current drinking habits, you could lose ten pounds or more simply by making water your primary beverage. One of my friends once lost over twenty-five pounds in six months just by cutting back on how much soda he was drinking.

What Else Can You Drink Besides Water?

Many people underestimate how many extra calories and unhealthy chemicals there are in other drinks. Let's look at four common beverage categories:

- *Milk.* If you choose to drink milk from animals, eatthis.com (America's most extensive source of nutrition information for restaurants and supermarket foods) recommends milk from organic, grass-fed animals, instead of animals that could be subject to hormones and antibiotics.[8] Grass-fed animals also have higher levels of omega-3's and CLA (which is good) than animals that are fed grain and corn. While animal milk is an excellent source of protein, some reports estimate that up to 75 percent of people have difficulty digesting it.[9] If you want to cut back on consumption of milk from animals, you could swap it out for unsweetened almond milk. If you do, eatthis. com recommends that you select a brand without carrageenan, an additive linked to a variety of gastrointestinal problems.[10]

- *Coffee.* If you choose to drink coffee, the healthiest option is to stick to one or two cups before lunch and take it black or only add the animal/almond milk options above. Many people add extra calories and chemicals onto their coffee habit by adding sugar and artificial creamers to each cup. Drinking too much coffee can lead to irritability, anxiety, or even a caffeine addiction. If you find that you are cranky or unable to perform optimally without coffee, this could be due to insufficient sleep, which might be due to drinking coffee in the first place. In one study led by Dr. Christopher L. Drake of Wayne State University, researchers found that caffeine consumed within six hours of bedtime led to significant disruptions in sleep quality and quantity, even among those who did not believe they were impacted.[11]

- *Carbonated beverages and sports drinks.* If you enjoy carbonated beverages, sparkling water (flavored naturally) is the healthiest option. Most people realize that regular soda and diet soda are unhealthy. However, many sports drinks and energy drinks are just as bad and contain as much sugar and as many artificial additives as soda. When you drink enough water and fuel yourself properly, there is no need for a sports drink during exercise lasting less than forty-five minutes. Either way, a healthier option during or after a tough workout is 100 percent coconut water.

- *Alcohol.* The unhealthiest adult beverages are the sugary ones. A frozen Margarita can easily contain over one hundred grams of sugar. If you choose to drink alcohol, an occasional glass of red wine is the best option. If you drink beer, light beers usually provide 33–50 percent fewer calories than regular beers.

Work Stronger Wisdom

"Your brain actually shrinks as you gain extra body weight. There are incredible benefits for your brain's health, resilience, and performance when you eat right."

—Dr. Daniel Johnston, co-founder at BrainSpan,
a brain health analytics company

STRONGER EATING HABIT #4: PREPARE (OR PURCHASE) FUEL IN ADVANCE

One of my co-workers often holds a thirty-minute window in his calendar around lunch time as a reminder to "eat something." There is a much greater likelihood that he will "eat something *healthy*" if he plans the meal in advance, instead of just deciding what to eat when his computer prompts him.

While there will never be consensus on a nutrition plan that everyone should follow, we can all agree on one thing. Every person needs to consume calories to survive and thrive. Why not plan ahead and prepare (or purchase) some of your fuel in advance, instead of always waiting until you are hungry to decide what to eat?

According to Dr. Brian Wansink (author of *Mindless Eating* and *Slim By Design*), the average person makes over two hundred decisions (not a typo) related to food every day.[12] When you prepare (or purchase) healthy fuel in advance, you will lower your number of total eating decisions, and you will increase your likelihood of making good choices.

How Can You Get Started with Meal Prep?

You can do meal prep daily (e.g., before or after work), or you can do it weekly (e.g., during a two- to three-hour window during the weekend). Some combination usually works best. Whatever you decide, be sure to hook your prep onto other activities in your schedule. Preparing your own food really consists of four steps, which you can complete as one routine, or as separate routines that are hooked onto activities on different times/days:

- Step 1: Decide what meals and snacks you want to prep.
- Step 2: Create a shopping list for the ingredients that you need.
- Step 3: Buy the ingredients.
- Step 4: Prepare your fuel.

If you are a novice in the kitchen, you could start by preparing one basic dish each weekend. The easiest option is a simple entrée in which all ingredients are cooked together, either in a crockpot on your counter, in a pot on your stove, or in a baking dish in your oven.

It usually takes about the same amount of time to prepare one serving of a dish as it does to prepare five to ten servings (or even more), so prepping meals in bulk is a good idea. When you cook in bulk, you can then store some meals in your fridge for the week, and store some in the freezer for later. If you plan to freeze food for later, let it cool off after cooking. Then, store individual meals in aluminum foil pans (or in separate freezer bags that can be flattened). This makes it easier to defrost and consume individual meals in the future.

Instead of preparing one-dish entrées, you could also prepare items individually. For example, you could prepare proteins (e.g., baked salmon, grilled chicken, hard-boiled eggs), fibrous carbs (e.g., quinoa, oats, sweet potatoes), or roasted/steamed vegetables (e.g., broccoli, asparagus, carrots). Then, you could mix and match these items during the week, while adding healthy fat (e.g., nuts, avocado, or olive oil) and other sources of flavor (e.g., fresh fruit, vinegar, salsa, or juice from limes or lemons) to create meals that feel and taste fresh.

As you get more comfortable in the kitchen, you can test out more complicated recipes, add more cooking sessions each week, or prepare more fuel each time that you cook. There are many ways to make cooking fun, which will help you overcome a potential obstacle of not wanting to cook. You could listen to music, you could listen to a sporting event in the background, or you could cook with friends or family.

One CEO even uses weekend meal prep as a way to raise awareness for his company and engage his customers and employees. Each Sunday, John Legere, CEO at T-Mobile USA, is filmed as he creates a quick meal using his magenta, custom-designed T-Mobile slow cooker.[13] The videos are broadcast through Facebook Live and promoted through other social media sites, including Twitter, where Legere has more than five million followers (as of 2018).

STRONGER EATING HABIT #5: READ BEFORE YOU EAT OR DRINK

Billions of dollars are spent each year by companies selling unhealthy products. According to a report by the Yale Rudd Center for Food Policy & Obesity, beverage companies spent $866 million in 2013 alone to advertise unhealthy drinks.[14]

Do not assume something is good for you just because it is endorsed by a famous person or organization. LeBron James has served as a spokesperson for Dunkin' Donuts, Peyton Manning has served as a spokesperson for Papa John's pizza, and Serena Williams has served as a spokesperson for Pepsi soda. Pro sports teams and leagues also sign sponsorship deals with similar businesses. The irony here is incredible.

In addition, do not assume something is good for you just because it sounds healthy. IHOP has a Chicken & Spinach Salad on its menu that contains over 2,200 mg of sodium.[15] That's about the same amount of sodium found in over two hundred Lay's potato chips.[16] Dannon and Yoplait each make yogurts with more than twenty grams of sugar in one serving.[17] That's about the same amount of sugar found in fifty Reese's Pieces.[18] Gatorade produces a protein bar with more sugar and a longer list of ingredients than a Snickers bar.[19]

What Should You Look for With Nutrition Labels?

Here are seven tips on how to read nutrition labels, so that you can make healthier choices:

1. *Beware of products with labels that scream.* Beware of products advertising that they are "low" or "free" of something

that is supposedly bad. Many items that are "low-fat," "fat-free," "sugar-free," "low-calorie," "calorie-free," "gluten-free," etc. have been heavily processed, stripped of nutrients, and filled with chemicals to enhance taste or shelf life.

2. *Avoid or limit products with science lab ingredients.* "Monosodium glutamate," "partially hydrogenated oil," "sodium phosphate," and other additives that you do not recognize should stay in the science lab and out of your stomach. Focus on fresh, minimally processed foods with short ingredient lists. Even better, select items with just one ingredient, like spinach, salmon, and avocadoes.

3. *Avoid or limit products with "added sugar" or sugar substitutes.* Starting in 2018, nutrition labels will begin to differentiate between "added sugar" and other forms of carbohydrates, so "added sugar" will be easier to spot. However, manufacturers often use sugar substitutes to get around this. Beware of foods with ingredients that you have never heard of before.

4. *Avoid or limit low-quality animal products.* If you can afford it, choose organic animal products as much as possible. Select fish that are wild (not farm-raised), and select meats from animals that are grass-fed (not grain-fed). These options will have more nutrients and be less likely to contain the artificial preservatives, hormones, and antibiotics that are often found in lower-quality animal products.

5. *Avoid or limit products that contain unhealthy fats.* You want to cut back on fried foods and items with trans fats or vegetable oils like corn, palm, soy, or sunflower oil, all of which are higher in inflammatory fat (omega-6) and lower in anti-inflammatory fat (omega-3).

6. *Avoid or limit products that are high in sodium.* High sodium intake can increase blood pressure and your risk of heart disease. The CDC recommends that you consume less than 2300 mg of sodium per day.[20] Certain populations, such as those who already have high blood pressure, should consume even less. Aim for foods and drinks that will keep each of your meals under 500 mg or so of sodium. (This restriction will rule out many products that are heavily processed.)

7. *Decode restaurant menus.* Beware of dishes that include mysterious sauces or words like battered, breaded, buttered, crisp, creamy, crusted, cured, fried, heavy, loaded, rich, or thick. Better menu options usually include words like baked, boiled, broiled, grilled, poached, roasted, or steamed.

STRONGER EATING HABIT #6: ENJOY TREATS GUILT-FREE

If you want to eat natural foods 100 percent of the time, more power to you. However, you can have your cake and be fit, too. You can also have pizza, ice cream, chocolate, or any other fattening product that you enjoy, as long as you are mindful about it.

There are two main ways in which you can enjoy treats. First, you can have what I refer to as *Scheduled Treats.* Some people find it simpler, more satisfying, and easier to stay on track by limiting treats to certain days and times (e.g., once a week or once a day). Instead of constantly having to determine if or how much you can indulge, you have clear boundaries and guidelines. Your favorite unhealthy items also become bigger treats, since you enjoy them less frequently. One risk, though, is the "I'd better make the most of it" mindset, in which you "over-treat" yourself, since you know you have to wait a while before your next chance.

Those who prefer not to indulge on a schedule might prefer what I refer to as *Flexible Treats.* With this approach, you try to eat natural foods for a certain percentage of the time (e.g., 80–90 percent), and you indulge when you are in the mood. One risk here is that your actual percentage of healthy consumption can skew much lower than you might realize. This approach also forces you to make more eating decisions every day, since you do not have the clear boundaries and guidelines of a more structured approach.

Whatever you prefer, if you plan to eat or drink something unhealthy, try to do it outside of your home. As discussed in chapter 4, storing unhealthy foods at home will lead to greater consumption of them.

You can also consider the advice provided by Dr. Michael Roussell in B.J. Gaddour's book titled *Men's Health Your Body Is Your Barbell*: "You can eat as much as you want at any given meal, but you need to be able to eat that same exact amount of food two to three hours later."[21] For example, if you want to indulge with pizza, eat two or three slices, not six. Based on personal experience, you will get virtually as much satisfaction, and your stomach will thank you.

FIVE STEPS TO CREATE YOUR PERFECT MEAL

Here is a step-by-step process on how to create *your* perfect meal, based on recommendations from Precision Nutrition (PN). Note: You can also download a number of free infographics from PN at http://www.precisionnutrition.com/blog/infographics.

Step 1: Start with Quality Protein

Protein keeps you fuller longer and helps you preserve and build muscle. PN recommends that men aim for two palm-sized servings per meal (about forty to sixty grams of protein), while women should aim for one palm-sized serving per meal (about twenty to thirty grams of protein).[22] Here are some examples of *one* serving size:

- Four ounces of meat
- Four ounces of fish
- Three to four whole eggs
- Six to eight egg whites
- One cup of plain, nonfat Greek yogurt
- One can of beans (Note: beans are also high in carbohydrates)
- One scoop of protein powder

Step 2: Add Nutrient-Dense Vegetables

Virtually all of us fail to meet the minimum recommendations for vitamins and minerals, which are necessary for proper functioning of your body and brain. Vegetables are full of many of these essential nutrients. Instead of providing you with a complex breakdown of which vegetables provide which vitamins and minerals, you will get a variety of nutrients if you simply eat fruits and vegetables of many different colors (i.e., green, blue, orange, red, and yellow).

PN recommends that men aim for two fist-sized servings of vegetables per meal, while women should aim for one fist-sized serving per meal.[23] Examples include kale, spinach, bell peppers, carrots, broccoli, or cauliflower.

Step 3: Add Fibrous Carbs

While many people consume way too many carbohydrates, extremely low-carb diets can decrease your metabolism and throw off your stress hormones and muscle-building hormones.[24] Avoid table sugar and heavily processed carbs (like breads, cereals, candy, crackers, and so on) as much as possible. Stick to natural, fibrous carbs, which will keep you fuller for longer and also provide steadier energy.

PN recommends that men aim for two cupped-hand sized servings per meal (about forty to sixty grams of carbohydrates), while women should aim for one cupped-hand sized serving per meal (about twenty to thirty grams of carbohydrates).[25] Here are some examples of *one* serving size for a fibrous carb:

- One apple, pear, or orange
- One-half cup of berries
- One sweet potato
- One-quarter cup of oats, quinoa, or brown rice

Step 4: Add Healthy Fat

While trans fats should be avoided and vegetable oils like corn, palm, soy, or sunflower oil should be limited, other (healthy) fats support a number of bodily functions and can help improve body composition.[26] PN recommends that men aim for two thumb-sized servings per meal (about fifteen to twenty-five grams of fat), while women should aim for one thumb-sized serving per meal (about seven to twelve grams of fat).[27] Here are some examples of *one* serving size of a healthy fat:

- One-half of an avocado
- One tablespoon of extra-virgin olive oil
- One tablespoon of nut butter
- Ten almonds or cashews

Step 5: Add Natural Flavor

PN recommends that you select ingredients from a regional flavor profile.[28] Here are five examples:

- Caribbean—allspice, cinnamon, cloves, or nutmeg
- French—bay leaf, lemon, rosemary, or thyme
- Indian—coriander, curry powder, ginger, or turmeric
- Italian—basil, capers, olives, or oregano
- Mexican—cilantro, cumin, or lime

The quantities recommended in steps one to four are starting points. Here are some extra tips from PN on customizing the suggestions for your situation:[29]

- You might want to *decrease* the carbohydrate and/or fat recommendations by 50 percent at some of your meals if you want to lose weight, if you are not very active, or if you eat more frequently.
- You might want to *increase* the carbohydrate and/or fat recommendations by 50 percent at some of your meals if you want to gain weight, if you are very active, or if you eat less frequently.

What Should You Eat Before and After a Workout?

In general, you can eat one of your standard meals one to two hours before your workout and one to two hours after your workout.[30] If you want to be more precise, you can adjust based on timing, your goals, and your exercise duration and intensity. For example, you might prefer a smaller and/or liquid meal if you have less than an hour to digest before exercise (e.g., if you work out first thing in the morning).

Your post-workout fueling strategy depends on what/when you eat before your workout, in addition to how long and intense your exercise session is. For example, you might want to consume *less* than one of your standard meals post-workout if you had a larger meal before exercise, or if your exercise session was less than thirty minutes and/or not that intense. You might want to consume *more* than one of your standard meals post-workout if you did not eat much before your workout, or if your workout was longer than thirty minutes and/or especially difficult. (Another post-workout approach is to drink a nutrient-dense protein/recovery drink right after a tough workout and then have one of your standard meals one to two hours after that.)

CHAPTER SUMMARY

Focus on habits, not diets. Different nutritional plans can be effective, as long as you primarily consume real foods with natural ingredients. This chapter highlighted six key eating habits that will help you feel and perform your best:

- Stronger eating habit #1: Wake up, fuel up
- Stronger eating habit #2: Re-fuel every three to four hours
- Stronger eating habit #3: Drink water, not calories or chemicals
- Stronger eating habit #4: Prepare (or purchase) fuel in advance
- Stronger eating habit #5: Read before you eat or drink
- Stronger eating habit #6: Enjoy treats guilt-free

Remember *the Headlights Method*. If you are not currently eating a natural, nutrient-dense breakfast on most days, you could start there and focus on that alone for now. Take it one change at a time, and add on the next change whenever you are ready. Here are some questions that you might want to ask yourself as you reflect on this chapter:

- How do you feel and perform when you eat well? How do you feel and perform when you don't eat well?
- What are your greatest obstacles in regard to your eating habits? How could you overcome these obstacles?
- Based on the recommendations in this chapter from Precision Nutrition (PN), what would a perfect breakfast/ meal look like for you? How could you tweak this meal to mix it up?

CHAPTER 7

SWEAT

Exercise is the single most powerful tool you have to optimize your brain function.
—Dr. John J. Ratey in *Spark: The Revolutionary New Science of Exercise and the Brain*[1]

An excerpt from a conversation I had at a party with a man named Ed:

Ed: Hey Pete, I hear you are a certified fitness trainer. Can you give me some advice?

Pete: Sure, happy to help.

Ed: I've been thinking about running a half-marathon in a few months, but...

Pete: But what?

Ed: But I hate running.

Pete: And you want to run a half-marathon?

Ed: Well, I want to tighten up and get into better shape. I figure this is the best way to do it...

There are many myths about exercise. Here are three of the most common:

- Myth #1: You need to torture yourself with activities that you find tedious.
- Myth #2: You need a ton of time to get fit.

- Myth #3: You should only do cardio if you want to lose weight or tone up, and you should only do strength training if you want to get bigger.

In this chapter, we'll tackle each of these fallacies, and others. You will also learn six essential exercise habits to get the best results for your body and brain in the least amount of time. Please check with your medical professional before starting an exercise program.

STRONGER EXERCISE HABIT #1: MAKE TIME

If you think that you are busy, imagine being CEO of a publicly traded internet company that provides non-stop, twenty-four/seven service to over 200 million active users, including A-list celebrities, the president of the United States, and the Pope. It would be easy for someone leading such an organization to claim that he was too busy to find time for exercise.

Dick Costolo, former CEO at Twitter

However, Dick Costolo, internet entrepreneur and former CEO at Twitter, found that strenuous exercise gave him the energy and resilience to overcome the relentless challenges that he faced running one of the world's top sources of breaking news and one of the most active, influential web sites on the planet. Dick *makes* time for exercise. "This is probably the best investment in yourself that you can make," he told me. "You'll get a much bigger return from twenty minutes of exercise than you will from another twenty minutes wading through emails or being in meetings."

The busier you are, the more important it is to be active. Saying you are too busy for exercise is like saying you are too busy to stop for gas because of how far you want to drive. Make time for exercise *because* you are busy. Exercise will make the rest of your day more productive, and it will make your brain stronger over the long term. When you approach exercise the right way, you do not need as much time as you might think anyway. (More to come on that later in this chapter.)

Work Stronger Wisdom

"Everyone is busy. You have to decide that your health and well-being will be a priority. This can't be something that you kind of do part of the time."

—Penny Pritzker, an entrepreneur, civic leader,
and philanthropist who also
served as US Secretary of Commerce
in the Obama administration

Exercise Provides Countless Benefits for Your Career

Studies have demonstrated that exercise provides a number of brain-boosting benefits, including greater creativity, a sharper memory, and a stronger ability to focus.[2] A study conducted at the University of Illinois at Urbana-Champaign even demonstrated that exercise can reverse cognitive decline associated with aging.[3]

The people interviewed for this book also gave me a number of additional reasons why they make time for exercise. Kristin Machacek Leary, chief human resources officer at Forcepoint (a global cybersecurity company), told me that exercise makes her tougher. "I work and travel so much for business, and I believe an active lifestyle has kept me resilient and not drained," she said.

Elliott Ferguson, president and CEO at Destination D.C., told me that exercise gives him more stamina. "A lot of people think that working out will make you tired, but it actually energizes you," he said.

Tom Lokar, CHRO at Mitel, told me that being fit gives him more confidence. "You realize that you have done things athletically that are harder than many of the challenges you face at work," he said.

Robin Thurston, CEO at Helix, told me that exercise helps him break away from work and technology. "The way I really disconnect is when I ride my bike," he said. "I fundamentally need it. I don't think I could operate at the level I need to without it."

Robin Thurston, CEO at Helix

How Much Should You Exercise Each Week?

The American College of Sports Medicine (ACSM), a global leader in sports medicine and exercise science, provides the following as weekly exercise recommendations for adults:[4]

- *Aerobic exercise*: At least 150 minutes of moderate-intensity (or at least sixty minutes of high-intensity) aerobic activity each week.
- *Strength training exercises* for all major muscle groups on at least two days each week.
- *Flexibility exercises* for all major muscle groups on at least two days each week.
- *Balance and coordination exercises* on at least two days each week.

You can meet these guidelines in about thirty minutes of exercise on five to six days a week. Anyone can set aside one half-hour each day (or most days). This is only 2 percent of your time. You do not need to start here though. This is simply what to aim for eventually.

Take a few minutes each weekend and schedule when you will exercise during the following week. Morning workouts are ideal since you have greater control over your schedule then, and they set a strong tone for your day. If you prefer to work out later on though, hook your training onto something else in your schedule, like your lunch hour or your commute home from work.

Just like there is no single diet that you must follow, there is no single workout regimen that you must follow. Customize your program based on your current fitness level, your interests, your goals, and your schedule. You can also tweak your routine and schedule daily, weekly, monthly, or seasonally.

What About Tracking Steps?

According to ACSM, tracking your steps with a pedometer or step-tracking device is "not an accurate measure of exercise quality and should not be used as the sole measure of physical activity."[5] If you enjoy tracking your steps, you can certainly do so. However, it's more important that you work toward meeting the guidelines that ACSM provides in regard to moderate/high-intensity aerobic activity, strength training, flexibility exercises, and balance/coordination exercises.

How Can You Get Started If You Are a Beginner?

Based on ACSM's recommendations, the eventual goal is to exercise at a moderate or high intensity for at least thirty minutes a day on five to six days each week. Do not feel badly or overwhelmed if you are not yet at that level. Few people are. Pending approval by a doctor, beginners can start with one of the following two options for the first few weeks:

- **Option 1:** Schedule a twenty to thirty minute moderate-intensity workout on one to two days per week, and schedule a twenty to thirty minute low-intensity workout (e.g., walking) on four to five other days.
- **Option 2:** Schedule a twenty to thirty minute moderate intensity workout on one to two days per week, but don't schedule anything officially for the other days.

You might prefer scheduling more exercise sessions each week (Option 1), since exercise becomes a habit faster and part of your daily schedule when you do it all/most days. If a daily habit feels overwhelming though, focus on a smaller frequency first. Then, you can gradually increase your frequency of moderate- or high-intensity workouts when you are ready.

> **Work Stronger Wisdom**
>
> "You might think you are too busy, but even thirty minutes of activity will propel you a few hours ahead in terms of energy level and creativity."
>
> —Kevin Hart, executive vice president and chief technology officer at Cox Communications (a broadband communications and entertainment company)

STRONGER EXERCISE HABIT #2: MAKE EXERCISE FUN

The sound system once stopped working for ten minutes while I was teaching a high-intensity exercise class. This is a group fitness instructor's worst nightmare. As I frantically fiddled with the stereo, one woman in class looked at me and said, "This is really boring without music." She is not the only person who feels that way.

Brunel University psychologist, Dr. Costas Karageorghis, has spent more than twenty years studying the relationship between music and exercise. His work has demonstrated that certain kinds of music can motivate you to train harder, faster, and longer. He says that the right music can increase endurance by as much as 15 percent and significantly reduce the perception of effort.[6]

His research has also shown that different kinds of music are better for different kinds of activity. Songs with a slower beat (eighty to 120 beats per minute) are generally better for warming up, cooling down, or exercising at a lesser intensity—when your heart rate will be lower. Songs with a faster beat (120–140 beats per minute) are generally better for exercising at a higher intensity—when your heart rate will be higher.[7]

If you do not want to be as scientific about it, you could simply listen to your favorite tunes, whatever they might be. Or...you could listen to books on tape. Or...you could listen to nothing. It's up to you, so do whatever will make the experience as enjoyable as possible for you.

In addition to audio, there are many other factors that you can tweak to make exercise fun. There are so many ways to be active, strong, and healthy. Mix it up and find out what works for you. Here are three other variables that you can adjust daily, weekly, monthly, or seasonally:

- **Where you exercise:** If you have not enjoyed going to a gym in the past, you might have been at the wrong one for you. Some gyms will feel more hardcore, while others will feel more like a spa. This creates a very different environment (socially and physically). Your experience can even change at separate clubs run by the same company, or at different times of day at the same club. You do not have to go to a gym though. Instead, you could exercise at home or outside at a track, trail, park, beach, or pool.

- **How you exercise:** If you do not enjoy running, you could go for a bike ride, jump rope, play basketball, or take a dance class. If you do not want to do strength training with barbells, you could use resistance bands, kettlebells, sand bags, or your own body weight. If you are overwhelmed or uninterested in designing your own workout, you could hire a trainer, take a group fitness class, use a fitness app, or follow a home workout program.

- **Who you exercise with:** If you do not enjoy exercising by yourself, you could exercise with friends, co-workers, family members, or even pets. Scott O'Neil, CEO at Harris Blitzer Sports & Entertainment (which includes the Philadelphia 76ers, the New Jersey Devils, and leading venue Prudential Center), has been organizing 6:00 a.m. pick-up basketball games for co-workers and business associates throughout his career. Don Monistere, president at TekLinks, told me that he lifts weights with his teenage son before they go to work/school every day. Barbara Tulipane, CEO at National Recreation and Park Association (NRPA), told me that she likes to run with her dog sometimes.

The more you enjoy being active, the more likely you will begin to crave exercise and turn it into a long-term habit. Do not confuse enjoyable with easy, however. Let's talk about that next.

STRONGER EXERCISE HABIT #3: MAKE EVERY SECOND COUNT

At most gyms and workout venues, you will find people hanging out, filling out crossword puzzles, or updating Instagram while they "exercise." If you want to get stronger—physically, mentally, and psychologically—a different approach and mindset is required. Once your workout begins, *make every second count.*

When you bring this level of focus, you can get powerful results in much less time than many people realize. Use every second of your workout time for strategic, focused movement (aerobic exercise, strength training, flexibility exercises, or balance exercises) or for strategic, focused rest periods that are used strictly to recover from the prior movement and to prepare for the movement to follow.

Your phone can be one of the biggest obstacles for making every second count. Ideally, you want to exercise without your phone, or keep it on airplane mode. In a 2016 study published in *Computers in Human Behavior*, one group of people was asked to work out without their phones, while another group texted during their workouts. Each group exercised for the same amount of time. The researchers found that those who texted during exercise spent more than three times as long in a low-intensity zone than those who exercised without their phones.[8]

How Can You Monitor Your Exercise Intensity?

You can make every second count whether you are a beginner or an elite athlete; your fitness level is irrelevant. Here are three ways to monitor your exercise intensity during a workout:

- **Sweat:** If you don't need a shower after your workout, did you really work out? While sweat should not be your only guide for moderate or high-intensity activity, it is one unsophisticated indicator recommended by ACSM.[9]
- **Your ability to talk:** In general, you are exercising at a moderate intensity if you can talk, but not sing during the activity. If you cannot say more than a few words without pausing for a breath, then you are exercising at a high intensity.[10]
- **Heart rate:** If you want to be more scientific, you can monitor your pulse (using a heart rate monitor or by taking your pulse manually) in relation to your maximum heart rate. The most precise method for determining your maximum heart rate is to get tested under the supervision of a cardiologist. A simpler (but less precise) method is to estimate your maximum heart rate by subtracting your age from 220. Keep in mind this estimate can be off by ten to twenty beats in either direction.

What's the Relationship between Heart Rate and Intensity?

Here are some guidelines on estimating your intensity based on your heart rate:

- Intensity is "low" when you are exercising below 60 percent of your max heart rate.

- Intensity is "moderate" when you are exercising at 60–75 percent of your max heart rate.
- Intensity is "high" when you are exercising at 75–100 percent of your max heart rate.

Note: Strength training (performed separately from cardiovascular activity) can still be very demanding without elevating your heart rate into the range associated with high-intensity training. (More to come on strength training later in this chapter.)

> **Work Stronger Wisdom**
> "Some people think you have to log a gigantic number of hours exercising, especially when you are training for an endurance race like an Ironman. Training is much more about quality than quantity though."
>
> —Frank Karbe, an executive recognized in 2005 and 2013 by CEO Challenges as "World's Fittest CEO"

Frank Karbe, CFO at Myovant Sciences

STRONGER EXERCISE HABIT #4: WARM UP, STAY WARM, COOL DOWN

It was a frigid December day in Washington, D.C. The wind chill was in the single digits. My flag football team was in a second-round playoff game.

After intercepting a pass at the back-right corner of the end zone, I launched into an all-out sprint down the right side of the field. In an attempt to cut me off around the fifty-yard line, the opposing quarterback was running toward the sideline. I cut back, and he ran right past me. All I had to do now was run straight ahead for another forty yards to the end zone.

I never made it though. One second later, I tore my hamstring. Did you hear it snap? It felt like a tennis ball was fired out of the back of my left leg. After a few hops on my right leg, I collapsed at the twenty-yard line.

This play occurred in the second game of a double-header. We had a twenty-minute break in between games. During that time, I sat on the sideline and hung out with my teammates. I figured I would warm-up again during the next game. Little did I know that I would be attempting a one-hundred-yard sprint a few moments later, while my body was ice cold.

Here are some tips on how to prevent your own injuries and maximize your workout results by warming up, staying warm, and cooling down:

Warm Up

A proper warm-up helps you prepare mentally for the exercise to follow, while also increasing your performance and reducing your chances of injury. Use the start of your workout as the cue to warm up for at least five minutes. The best warm-up is a lower-intensity version of the exercise that you plan to do that day.

Start slow and easy, build gradually, and target your entire body, or at least the major muscles that you plan to use that day. If you are going for a light jog on a hot day, your warm-up might only need to be a few minutes and can be pretty simple. However, a higher intensity workout (e.g., sprints or intense strength training) requires a longer, more strategic warm-up (generally at least eight to ten minutes). Can you skip or shorten the warm-up if you are in a rush? Nope.

If your time is limited, warm up anyway. Then, train harder and use your time more efficiently during your workout.

Stay Warm

You can erase the benefits of a great warm-up if you get cold later in your workout. The right clothing can help you stay warm, especially if you are training in cold weather or in a cold indoor location. Compression shirts, shorts, sleeves, or tights can be very helpful, and they feel great, too.

Cool Down

Inevitably, there are a number of people who leave one of my high-intensity exercise classes immediately after the difficult part of the workout ends. That's like driving seventy miles per hour and jamming on your brakes as hard as you can, which is great for crash test dummies and not so great for real people.

Your cool-down should be the opposite of your warm-up. Reduce your intensity gradually. Focus on stretching each major muscle in your body, or at least the primary muscles that you used that day. Take some time to acknowledge what you did for yourself, to slow down, and to enter a more peaceful state before you move on with your day.

STRONGER EXERCISE HABIT #5: FOCUS ON SIX KEY MOVEMENTS EACH WEEK

Imagine that you get up one morning and go to make your bed. You tossed and turned a lot the night before, so your bed sheets are all wrinkled. You really want the center of your sheets to be tight, so you try to smooth out the middle of your bed. You do not tuck in any other area though. You ignore the corners and sides. What would happen? The sheets would not get tight in the middle, or anywhere else.

Now, imagine what would occur if you tucked in the sheets at every corner and side of the bed—the left side, the right side, the front, the back, and the corners. Every single inch. As you tucked in each additional area, the middle of your bed sheets would get tighter and tighter.

While this is not what happens with your body during an exercise, this is a good image to keep in mind. Train your entire body, even if you only want to tighten up one body part. You cannot spot-reduce anyway. If you are skeptical, prove it to yourself. Have you ever seen someone with a tight stomach and flabby arms or legs?

Training your entire body each week is easier than it might sound. While there are hundreds of different exercises that you could do, the following six key movements (which I refer to collectively as *The Stronger Six*) will target every major muscle group (your heart, legs, chest, shoulders, back, arms, and core) and help you get the best results in the least amount of time:

- **Elevate**: This is a catch-all term that I use to refer to any exercise that increases your heart rate and makes you perspire. This includes cardiovascular activities like running, cycling, or swimming. You could also "elevate" and work on your balance or coordination at the same time by jumping rope, boxing, or dancing. Or, you could "elevate" and do resistance training together by combining some or all of the other key movements in a heart-pumping circuit. If time is limited, this is a very efficient approach.

- **Squat**: In this lower-body exercise, you begin from a standing position and bend at your knees and hips. This movement primarily strengthens the front of your legs (quadriceps) and your glutes, although you also use many additional muscles during this movement.

- **Hinge**: Credit for this term goes to Lou Schuler and Alwyn Cosgrove in their book *The New Rules of Lifting Supercharged: Ten All-New Programs for Men and Women*.[11] The most common example of the "hinge" movement is a deadlift, in which you lift weight off the ground to the level of your hips. An alternative to deadlifts is to do hamstring curls on a stability ball. The hinge movement is generally recognized for strengthening the back of your legs (hamstrings and glutes), although you also use many additional muscles during a deadlift.

- **Push:** In this upper-body exercise, you either push your body off the floor (as with push-ups), or you push a weight away from you (as with a dumbbell chest press or shoulder press). This movement primarily strengthens your chest, shoulders, and triceps.
- **Pull:** In this upper-body exercise, you either pull your body toward a bar or other object (as with pull-ups) or you pull weight toward you (as with dumbbell rows). This movement primarily strengthens your back and biceps.
- **Plank:** In this core strengthening exercise, you hold your body in a fixed position (as with a front plank or a side plank).

There are countless ways to tweak *The Stronger Six*, based on your goals, your current fitness level, and your desired level of difficulty. If you want to add other exercises beyond these each week, you certainly can, but start with these. Some people spend all of their exercise time on low-intensity cardio or supposed "toning" exercises, while neglecting the six key movements that will actually yield the greatest results in the least amount of time.

In general, you can elevate your heart rate on consecutive days. However, you want to leave at least one day in between doing the other movements, especially when you add resistance beyond your body weight. Muscle growth and repair occurs during recovery. Over-training can occur when you do not give your body proper time to heal between workouts. Along those lines, another good rule of thumb is to dial back your training for one week every two to three months. This further reduces your chances of over-training.

STRONGER EXERCISE HABIT #6: ALWAYS KEEP YOUR FORM FIRST

Many people sacrifice their technique to lift heavier, longer, or faster. Do not make this mistake. Always keep your form first. The alternative is simply not worth the risk, especially when you are not trying to win a powerlifting contest.

Beware of modeling your form after other people, even those who appear to be fit. Many people are either confused on what counts as proper form, or they are more focused on weight, speed, and reps.

Not sure if your form is on point? You can watch your technique in a mirror, or you can get help from a *Credible Coach*. Here are a few extra tips as well:

- Control any weight that you lift at all times. Using momentum will allow you to lift heavier, but it's dangerous and defeats the purpose of an exercise. Take at least one to two seconds in either direction per rep, with a brief a pause in the middle.
- Keep your neck and spine in a neutral position during any strength training movement. Common mistakes include dropping your neck or allowing your hips to sag (very common with push-ups and planks) and arching or rounding your back (very common when people hinge or do a pulling exercise).
- Remember to keep breathing as well. Sounds very obvious, but I can't tell you how often people in one of my classes forget to breathe! It can be easy to forget this when you are exercising at a high intensity.

WHY SHOULD YOU DO STRENGTH TRAINING?

According to 2016 data from the CDC, less than 22 percent of US adults meet the average weekly recommendations for strength training.[12] One cause of this is the myth that strength training will make you "bulky or "too musclebound." In reality, you get bulky from poor nutrition and/or poor sleep. You get too musclebound by eating an enormous amount of food, by doing strength training with a much higher volume of sets and reps than what is recommended later in this chapter, or by taking drugs or questionable supplements.

When combined with proper sleep and the right nutrition program, strength training makes you tighter and leaner, not thicker and bulkier. Strength training also improves your posture, reduces and prevents injuries and chronic aches, improves your body composition, builds up your bones and joints, preserves your muscle, and delays your aging process.

It's been estimated that we lose 8 percent of our muscle each decade starting at the age of forty, and that we start losing even more later in life.[13] According to Dr. Jeffrey Stout, a professor at the

University of Central Florida and a Fellow of the American College of Sports Medicine, the best ways to defend against this are by strength training and eating a protein-filled diet. "The more muscle mass you have, the better your life is going to be [as you age]," he said.[14]

The benefits of strength training came up during many of my interviews for this book. One excellent example is Rhonda Germany-Ballintyn, a female executive who lost over one hundred pounds (after the age of fifty) by lifting heavy weights. Rhonda told me that she "did not lose one ounce" when her exercise consisted of walking over twenty-five miles a week.

Rhonda Germany-Ballintyn, retired chief strategy and marketing officer at Honeywell

It was not until she started strength training and exercising at higher intensities that her body transformed. "When I started squatting and lifting heavy, that's when my dress size really dropped. Now, I'm a size two," she said. "It's all due to nutrition and lifting heavy weights. I now use dumbbells that weigh twenty-five to thirty pounds or more for just about every exercise that I do. I also do plyometrics [exercises designed to increase athleticism and explosiveness] and 100-meter sprints two times a week. It's amazing how much stronger and fitter I am now."

Many endurance athletes fear that strength training will make them bigger and negatively impact their race times. If you enjoy long cardio sessions, feel free to keep doing them (see exercise habit #2). However, you are asking for problems if you avoid strength training.

Small business owner Kent Wuthrich learned this the hard way. He got to the point where he was running forty to fifty miles each week, and he paid the price of being one-dimensional with his workout regimen. "I was able to get into the top 5–10 percent at races, but I kept getting hurt and had to deal with tendinitis and other ailments," he told me. "I also looked skinny and not healthy and strong. In my late thirties, I changed my approach and how I defined fitness. These days, I do a lot more weight training. My body composition has definitely changed for the better, and I feel much stronger."

Answers to Common Questions About Strength Training

- **What kind of equipment should you use?** Free weights activate more muscle and require greater coordination than machines. If you do not want to use barbells, dumbbells, or kettlebells, you can stick to resistance bands or body weight training.
- **How many reps should you do per set?** A good rule of thumb is to use enough resistance (using body weight, free weights, resistance bands, etc.) where you can only complete ten to twelve reps safely per set. You can do fewer than ten reps per set (with more resistance) if you want to focus more on strength and power. You can do twelve to twenty reps per set (with less resistance) if you want to focus more on endurance.
- **How many sets should you do?** Whatever rep range you choose, four to six total sets each week is a good guideline for each of the major strength training movements (squat,

hinge, push, pull). As for planks, four to six sets (thirty to sixty seconds per set) is also a good weekly target.

- **How long should you rest in between sets?** When you are in the ten- to twelve-rep range, one to two minutes is a good amount of time to rest between sets. If you do fewer than ten reps (with more resistance), you will likely need to rest for two to three minutes (maybe even more) between sets. If you do twelve to twenty reps (with less resistance), you can generally keep rest periods to one minute or less. Rest periods can be used as pure breaks, for stretching, or for other exercises that target different muscles.

FAST AND UNSTEADY

High-intensity interval training (HIIT) involves periods of intense effort (exercising at 75–100 percent of your maximum heart rate) followed by varied recovery periods. High-intensity intervals can last anywhere from a few seconds to a few minutes. Recovery periods are generally two to three times as long. For example, you could sprint for fifteen seconds and then recover for thirty to forty-five seconds. During that time, you could either jog at a much slower pace, or you could take a pure break. While HIIT workouts can be flat-out painful, they provide tremendous benefits. Pending your doctor's approval, there are many reasons to give them a try.

HIIT Builds Resilience and Toughness

Doing this sort of exercise a few times a week can transform you into a radically different person—in a good way. I've experienced this myself and witnessed it firsthand with many people who I've coached. As Dr. John J. Ratey writes in *Spark*, "High-intensity exercise toughens you up physiologically and psychologically."[15]

HIIT Is Extremely Efficient

Short on time? This kind of training is a very efficient way to burn calories, blast body fat, improve body composition, and enhance your overall health and fitness. In one experiment, scientists at McMaster University in Ontario demonstrated that five minutes of interval training (consisting of only sixty seconds of strenuous exercise) can yield the same physiological benefits as forty-five minutes of steady, less intense exercise.[16]

HIIT Is the Ultimate Stress-Reliever

Unlike easier kinds of physical activity (when you can ruminate about work or other topics), the demands of HIIT workouts make it virtually impossible to think about anything else. This benefit was mentioned by many of the people who I interviewed for this book. For example, Jennifer Carr-Smith, a SVP at Groupon, told me that she enjoys exercise that is so intense that it will make her stop thinking about work. "These kinds of workouts are great for stress relief," she said.

Dick Costolo, former CEO at Twitter, told me something similar. "When you are in the middle of a crazy, hardcore workout that you are trying to get done in twenty minutes, you simply can't think of anything else," he said. "You're just trying to finish. These kinds of workouts prevent you from obsessing about work or anything else. It's very different from when you go for a jog and your mind can still wander."

How Can You Get Started with HIIT?

You can design your own HIIT workouts, you can use a fitness app, or you can take HIIT classes, such as those offered at Orangetheory Fitness (OTF), a unique group personal training workout backed by the science of EPOC (excess post-exercise oxygen consumption). During EPOC, your body works to restore itself to pre-exercise levels. Training at a higher intensity results in a greater oxygen debt and requires your body to work harder post-exercise to get back to its normal state. Translation: High-intensity exercise also burns a lot of calories *after* your workout, not just during your workout.

Each sixty-minute OTF class trains your whole body and utilizes a variety of cardiovascular equipment, functional equipment, and strength training equipment. The entire hour is challenging and consists of a series of timed interval training blocks. At least twelve minutes of the hour is intended to get you into what OTF calls the "orange zone" (when your heart rate is at 84–91 percent of your max) or the "red zone" (when your heart rate is at 92–100 percent of your max). OTF's web site states that their program design can lead to an increased metabolic rate for up to thirty-six hours after the workout.[17]

Since HIIT is so intense, you need to pay extra attention to your nutrition and hydration before, during, and after these kinds of workouts. Proper recovery in between workouts is also important. Doing HIIT too often or for too long can be dangerous and counter-productive. Dave Long, OTF's CEO, told me that "a good rule of thumb is taking a day off in between workouts of this sort of intensity. You can do less intense activities on those days."

Work Stronger Wisdom

"You can actually stimulate brain growth through high-intensity exercise, which usually also helps people sleep better and improves mood and appetite as well."

—Dr. Daniel Johnston, co-founder at BrainSpan,
a brain health analytics company

THE 3-MINUTE CIRCUIT

Really short on time and looking for an effective, full-body workout that you can do anywhere? Give *the 3-Minute Circuit* a try. Just follow these four steps:

Step 1: Set up. Create your circuit for the day by selecting one variation of each movement in *The Stronger Six*. Grab a stopwatch and any necessary equipment as well. The following is one example. (Note: The order of the movements here is very intentional.)

- *Elevate*: Jog in place
- *Pull*: Resistance band rows
- *Squat*: Body weight squats
- *Push*: Body weight push-ups
- *Hinge*: Stability ball hamstring curls

- *Plank*: Front plank
- *Equipment required*: stopwatch, stability ball (to hinge), resistance band (to pull)

Step 2: Warm up. Aim for five to seven minutes.

Step 3: Work out. Complete your *3-Minute Circuit* three times in a row, as follows. If possible, rest only ten seconds between exercises and between circuits:

- *Elevate* for twenty seconds. (Then rest for ten seconds.)
- *Pull* for twenty seconds. (Then rest for ten seconds.)
- *Squat* for twenty seconds. (Then rest for ten seconds.)
- *Push* for twenty seconds. (Then rest for ten seconds.)
- *Hinge* for twenty seconds. (Then rest for ten seconds.)
- *Plank* for twenty seconds. (Then rest for ten seconds.)

Step 4: Cool down and stretch. Aim for five to seven minutes.

There are countless ways to tweak *the 3-Minute Circuit* by plugging in different variations of each movement or by adjusting the difficulty. A beginner could get a great workout using only their body weight, a resistance band (to pull), and a stability ball (to hinge). Someone who is fitter and stronger could use free weights to add more resistance for some or all of the movements.

Note: A pdf for *the 3-Minute Circuit* is included in *The Work Stronger Workbook* that you can download at WorkStronger.com.

CHAPTER SUMMARY

The best workout regimen for your body and brain is one that includes different intensities and a mixture of aerobic exercise, strength training, flexibility exercises, and balance/coordination exercises. This chapter highlighted six essential exercise habits to help you feel and perform your best:

- Stronger exercise habit #1: Make time
- Stronger exercise habit #2: Make exercise fun
- Stronger exercise habit #3: Make every second count

- Stronger exercise habit #4: Warm up, stay warm, cool down
- Stronger exercise habit #5: Focus on six key movements each week
- Stronger exercise habit #6: Always keep your form first

Remember *the Headlights Method*. If you are a beginner, you don't need to aim for ACSM's weekly exercise recommendations right away. Start as small as necessary, and make sure you feel at least 90 percent confident that you can follow through on what you have in mind. Increase your duration, frequency, or intensity whenever you are ready. Here are some questions that you might want to ask yourself as you reflect on this chapter:

- How do you feel and perform when you are making time for exercise? How do you feel and perform when you are not making time for exercise?
- What are your greatest obstacles in regard to exercise? How could you overcome these obstacles?
- What could you do to make exercise fun? How could you tweak your workout routine to keep it fresh and get better results?

CHAPTER 8

FOCUS

Focus like a laser, not a flashlight.
— Michael Jordan, six-time NBA champion

Work can be a source of energy, intellectual stimulation, and personal satisfaction. Work can also be a way to add value to society and make the world a better place. However, we are not robots that are capable of working at full capacity for twenty-four hours a day. At some point, working longer becomes counter-productive.

Research has demonstrated that working fewer hours can actually increase productivity. Harvard Business School's Leslie A. Perlow and Jessica L. Porter have conducted surveys and research on the work habits of people working in professional services—including occupations such as lawyers, accountants, and consultants. Their surveys have indicated that many of these individuals work more than sixty-five hours each week, in addition to spending more than twenty additional hours each week monitoring emails outside the office.[1]

Perlow and Porter set out to see what would happen if professional services employees worked shorter, more predictable hours. They conducted research over a four-year period with several North American offices of the Boston Consulting Group, a prestigious management consulting firm. They found that shorter, more predictable work hours actually increased productivity among teams of consultants, while also increasing overall career and life satisfaction.[2]

When your time at work is limited, it naturally becomes a more valuable resource that must be invested more carefully. Someone who has decided to leave work at 5:00 p.m. has to structure her schedule differently and bring a higher level of focus and prioritization to each hour than someone who has decided to work "as long as necessary." Shorter, more consistent work hours serve as tighter deadlines that focus you on higher-value activities. They encourage you to delegate and leverage the time and talents of other people, and they discourage you from wasting time on tasks that add little value or that could be performed by someone else.

While this entire book is designed to help you get the most out of each hour, this chapter focuses specifically on your behavior at work. You will learn three stronger work habits that will help you produce higher-quality work in much less time and with much less stress. You will also learn how to maximize your travel time, so you can be at least as productive (maybe even more productive) when you are on the road.

> **Work Stronger Wisdom**
> "I always ask myself, 'What will have the biggest impact?' I want to make sure that every hour is as effective as possible."
> —Janine Allis, founder of Boost Juice, author of
> *The Accidental Entrepreneur*, and
> investor on *Shark Tank*

STRONGER WORK HABIT #1: FOCUS ON ONE TASK AT A TIME

Imagine two women named Fran and Debra who each decide one afternoon to go for a three-mile run near their office. They each plan to run by themselves. They are each capable of completing this distance in thirty minutes.

Fran gets changed at her office, warms up for five minutes and departs on her run at 2:00 p.m. She is in the zone the entire time and finishes slightly faster than usual, at 2:29 p.m.

Debra gets changed, warms up, and departs at the same time, but her run ends up quite differently. Four minutes after she starts, she stops to respond to a text from a friend. Six minutes after that, she stops to speak with a co-worker who is also out for a run. Seven minutes after that, she stops to respond to an unexpected call from another co-worker. As a result, her run takes over an hour to finish.

Fran's run is your workday when you focus intensely on one task at a time. Debra's run is your workday when you try to multitask and allow yourself to be disrupted by incoming messages, office drop-ins, and unscheduled phone calls.

Research has demonstrated that trying to multitask makes you slower, not faster. For example, one study analyzed what happened when a group of Microsoft employees were interrupted by emails or instant messages. On average, the workers took fifteen minutes to get back to important tasks each time that they were disturbed, as the distractions generally led them to reply to other messages and/ or to visit various web sites unrelated to the task that they had been focused on before the distraction.[3]

Other research has demonstrated that multitasking could change your brain and make it even harder for you to be able to focus in the future. In other words, chronic multitasking trains your brain to be distracted. A study by the University of Sussex compared the brains of "media multitaskers" (people who used multiple media devices at the same time) with the brains of those who only use one device occasionally. While the study demonstrated a link and not causality, they found the multitaskers had lower gray-matter density in a part of the brain that is responsible for various cognitive and emotional control functions.[4]

So, how you can concentrate on one task at a time in a world with endless distractions? First of all, you can wear headphones at work. If you work in an open environment (or have an office with a glass door), this is a subtle, polite, and effective way to tell people not to interrupt you. Listening to peaceful music can also block out background noise around you and help you focus more intensely.

Another option for people without full-time access to a private office is to find what I refer to as an *Occasional Office* for use during times when you really do not want to be disturbed. This could be an unused room in your office building or a location outside your office, like a home office, a local library, or a quiet area of a hotel lobby. In a prior job, I often used one of my company's empty conference rooms during periods when I really needed to concentrate. In addition to helping you get away from the usual distractions in your standard workspace, an *Occasional Office* can also provide a nice change of scenery. While some companies may not allow this, it's worth looking into or asking for permission every now and then.

Wherever you work, you can also keep your email and social media accounts closed, and keep your phone off, on airplane mode, or simply not accessible during periods when you want to concentrate. In fact, why not make that your default setting at work? This idea might sound outrageous to you if you are used to being glued to your phone and email all day long. However, unless your primary job responsibility is to support someone else, your performance is probably measured by much more important metrics than your email response time. While some roles (like an executive assistant) may truly need to be available by email for virtually every minute of the workday, chances are that your position does not require or truly reward such behavior.

How many incoming emails and calls really need to be handled within seconds? You could still check your inboxes and devices every thirty or sixty minutes, if you feel compelled to do so. What you do not want to do is leave them open, buzzing, notifying, and interrupting you all day long.

Research has found that checking email less frequently can also reduce your stress. In one study, scientists at the University of British Columbia asked a group of people to check their email as often they could for one week. During another week, the participants in the experiment were asked to limit themselves to three email sessions. The researchers found that participants were significantly less stressed and felt much better overall during the week when they restricted their email time.[5]

Keeping your inbox and devices closed, off, or not easily accessible is another example of removing the cue, a strategy that we discussed in chapter 3. In this case, the cue is an incoming email, text, notification, or call that triggers a bad habit to break your concentration and deal with the message immediately. Rather than try to resist the temptation to read and respond to an incoming message, why not remove the temptation altogether?

You can try to multitask, or you can focus. You cannot do both. More than once while finishing the manuscript for this book, my brother left me a voicemail complaining that my phone was off and that this made it impossible to reach me live. Each time that I called him back, I reminded him that was the point.

> **Work Stronger Wisdom**
> "Phones are great tools, but many people are slaves to their phones. You want your phone to be a slave to you."
> —Scott O'Neil, CEO at Harris Blitzer Sports & Entertainment

STRONGER WORK HABIT #2: PLAN YOUR DAY IN ADVANCE

Have you ever looked at the clock at 5:00 p.m. and wondered where the day went? Have you ever felt like all or most of your day was wasted on minutiae instead of truly important activities? Have you ever worked eight to ten hours (or more) only to realize that your most important task for the day is still not finished?

Working off a big to-do list can lead to "one of those days," and it can encourage you to work longer, not stronger. To-do lists typically arrange tasks in a random order. This can tempt you to spend too much time on activities that are easy or enjoyable, instead of tasks that add the most value and that might be difficult or not as much fun. Either way, the first item on your to-do list might be the least important, while the seventh item on your list might be the most important. Since to-do lists usually include *at least* ten to twenty tasks, they also set you up for stress. A long list feels overwhelming. In addition, there's a psychological cost when you reach the end of the day and still have a bunch of incomplete items. Finally, since to-do lists usually do not quantify how long each task will take, a typical to-do list could actually include a week's worth of work, or even more. That's not a recipe for success or for sanity.

To be clear, a to-do list does have value. It is helpful to have one document (or one document per project) that serves as a master "storage bin" for all of your ideas and reminders and the tasks that you eventually need to complete. However, you do not want to go through your day by working off such a list. What should you do instead? Once again, that brings us back to *the Headlights Method.*

Applying the Headlights Method at Work

At the end of each week, review your long-term goals and ask yourself what you want to accomplish by the end of the following week. You could complete this weekly activity on Friday afternoons, on Saturday or Sunday mornings, or on Sunday nights. Then (and only then) are you well-positioned to establish your top priorities for a given day.

> **Work Stronger Wisdom**
>
> "Every Sunday—usually in the evening—I look at my calendar and try to figure out the most important things I have to get done over the next week. I ask myself, 'What do I absolutely have to get done by Friday or Saturday?' That drives my priorities for the week, and I refer back to this to establish my daily priorities."
>
> —Chip Bergh, president and CEO at
> Levi Strauss & Co.

The Work Stronger Day Planner is a one-page peak productivity tool that helps you identify your daily priorities—after you have determined what you want to accomplish for the week. This tool places tasks into three unique categories (*Scheduled Commitments, Reminders and Fast Tasks,* and *Unscheduled Priorities*). A pdf for *The Work Stronger Day Planner* is included in *The Work Stronger Workbook* that you can download at WorkStronger.com. To create your plan for a given day, follow these three steps:

- **Step 1: Identify your *Scheduled Commitments* for the day.** These are calls and meetings that were previously scheduled on your calendar. Note: Whether these calls or meetings are truly the best use of your time is a separate question that is not easily answered here.

- **Step 2: Identify your *Reminders and Fast Tasks* for the day.** These are activities that you can complete in fewer than fifteen minutes (e.g., "send contract to Chris" or "call Mary back"). This category serves as a daily "storage bin" for anything personal or professional that could slip through the cracks.
- **Step 3: Identify, quantify, and rank three *Unscheduled Priorities* for the day.** These high-value activities are important, but not urgent or scheduled. They are usually tasks to be completed on your own, such as preparing for presentations, reviewing contracts, or writing articles. You can identify your top *Unscheduled Priorities* by asking yourself this question several times: "If I only had one more hour outside of my *Scheduled Commitments*, what would be the most valuable way for me to use that hour?"

Depending on how much of your day is tied up with *Scheduled Commitments*, you generally want to identify your top three *Unscheduled Priorities* (thirty to sixty minutes each) to complete each day. If you have time after you finish all of them, you can then identify another high-value activity to tackle at that point. You can use larger chunks of open time in your day for *Unscheduled Priorities*, while only dealing with emails and *Reminders and Fast Tasks* when you have a few spare minutes, like when a call or meeting ends early. Instead of scheduling every minute of your day, leave yourself at least one to two hours for the unexpected.

Many *Unscheduled Priorities* cannot be finished in one hour, and you might not always know in advance how much time you will eventually need to complete a high-value activity. For example, you might ultimately need five hours to prepare for an upcoming presentation. Instead of writing "prepare for presentation" on your daily plan (what usually happens when you just work off a to-do list), *The Work Stronger Day Planner* helps you break down bigger projects and tasks into smaller, quantifiable increments and sub-tasks.

There are many benefits of this approach. First of all, smaller tasks are less intimidating. Secondly, this approach also allows you to experience a sense of completion throughout the day, which provides a psychological boost. Finally, it is usually much easier to fit *Unscheduled Priorities* into your calendar for thirty to sixty minutes at a time, instead of longer periods of time.

Block out time each day/week for *Unscheduled Priorities*. You can use these calendar slots as placeholders that will be filled in later, or you can decide in advance how you want to use them. Otherwise, you might end up with little or no time for these important activities. For example, in a survey conducted by The Energy Project and *Harvard Business Review*, less than 20 percent of their 19,000+ respondents reported that they consistently allocated time in their calendar for strategic and creative thinking.[6]

You can use the end of each day as a cue to create your plan for the following day. This ritual helps you bring closure to your workday, and it also helps you hit the ground running the next morning.

Work Stronger Wisdom

"Time management is about more than just allotting time. It's also about being disciplined with how you use that time. I spend my time focusing on the actions that will provide the most leverage. I ask myself 'What can I uniquely do that others in the organization cannot do?' Then, I do my best to empower people to do the other things."

—Penny Pritzker, an entrepreneur, civic leader, and philanthropist who also served as US Secretary of Commerce in the Obama administration

STRONGER WORK HABIT #3: WORK LIKE AN ATHLETE

At the start of my career, I never took breaks or left the office during the day. I worked for hours at a time, only stopping for a few minutes to eat lunch quickly at my desk. At the time, I thought this was the way to be successful. However, I had an epiphany later in my career, while teaching a high-intensity interval training (HIIT) class.

As you know from chapter 7, HIIT leads to more powerful results and requires less total time than training at a slower, steadier pace without breaks. One day, it hit me: *"Why don't I work like I train at the gym?"* This has been my approach at work ever since. Instead of working for hours at a time, you can increase your energy throughout the day and produce higher-quality output (in less time) when you work in intervals and fluctuate between periods of intense focus, followed by strategic "recovery" periods, which I refer to as *Boost Breaks*.

Take Boost Breaks

Boost Breaks are strategic, five- to ten-minute breaks that are designed to boost your energy quickly and naturally, so that you can work stronger during your next period of focus. Do not use *Boost Breaks* to check emails or to do other tasks that can sap your energy. Use them to stand up, perform light stretches, hydrate with some water, re-fuel with a healthy snack, or go for a brief walk (even better if you can get outside for that walk). In one study, researchers at the University of Georgia found that ten minutes of low-intensity activity (the kind that does not lead to sweating or requiring a shower) could make participants feel more energized than consuming 50 mg of caffeine, the amount found in a typical can of soda.[7]

There's a lot of additional research supporting the power of breaks. For example, the survey by The Energy Project and *Harvard Business Review* (referenced earlier in this chapter) found that those who take at least a brief break every ninety minutes reported a 28 percent higher level of focus than those who only take one break or no breaks during the day. In addition, The Energy Project found that those who take breaks reported their capacity to think creatively as being 40 percent greater and their health and well-being as 30 percent greater.[8]

Another study on breaks found that performance improved most when people worked for fifty-two minutes consecutively, and then took a break away from their desk and computer for seventeen minutes.[9] The concept of a break (and the way that you use the break) is more important than the specific duration though. You could follow a different focus/recovery ratio. For example, Elon Musk, the co-founder, CEO, and product architect at Tesla, follows the Pomodoro Technique, in which you focus for twenty-five minutes and then take a five-minute break.[10]

It's up to you how rigid you want to be with your focus/recovery ratio. There might be situations when you focus intensely for forty-five minutes and then take a fifteen-minute *Boost Break* before resuming or moving onto another project. Other times, you might focus intensely for sixty minutes and take a five-minute *Boost Break* before diving back in for another sixty minutes. This is a much more effective way to go through your day than trying to "power through" for hours at a time.

Make the Most Out of Half-time

To work like an athlete, you need to take breaks and you also need to make the most out of half-time: your lunch break. A 2012 survey conducted by Right Management (a brand of ManpowerGroup) found that less than 20 percent of employees take a real lunch break that includes time away from their desk.[11]

There are many ways that you can use your half-time as an extended *Boost Break* to increase your energy, decrease your stress, and enhance your performance. For example, David Inns, CEO at GreatCall (the leader in connected health for active aging), told me that he uses his lunch break to re-fuel with healthy food and to exercise on-site with employees.

If you do not want to sweat and shower midday, you could use lunch to re-fuel and to go for a walk. This is a great way to bring closure to the first half of the day and to get energized for a productive second half. You could also use a few minutes during or right after lunch to review your *Work Stronger Day Planner* for the rest of the day. If you feel overwhelmed (going into lunch or at any other time of day), use that emotion as a cue to step back and adjust your schedule or strategy.

If you are falling behind, you can look to the sports world for inspiration. Down 21-3 at halftime and down 28-3 in the second half, the New England Patriots completed one of the greatest comebacks in NFL history by defeating the Atlanta Falcons 34-28 in Super Bowl

LI. The lesson here is that you can still finish strong, even if you get off to a slow start or your initial game plan does not work.

TRAVEL LIKE A PRO
Time away from your main work location can be a source of stress and lost productivity, if you allow it to be. Travel does not always go as expected, and it will be uncomfortable unless you plan ahead. Here are seven recommendations to help you make the most of any time on the road:

Plan for Delays
According to the Bureau of Transportation Statistics, over 16 percent of all flights are delayed each year.[12] Why not build in extra time for potential schedule changes that are out of your control?

For example, Daniel Houghton, CEO at Lonely Planet (the world's leading travel media company), recommends giving yourself at least two hours for layovers between connecting flights. Thanks to this strategy, he has never missed a flight due to a missed connection.[13] He has also never had to deal with the stress of worrying if he will make a tight transfer.

Maximize Transit Time
Sure, you could just hang out or watch movies on your tablet, but what about using travel time for higher-value activities (e.g., strategic planning, reading, meditating, etc.) that might be difficult to squeeze in at home? Reading is my go-to activity during travel. If there are delays, no big deal. More time to read.

Make Transit More Comfortable
If you plan to sleep on a flight, bring a travel pillow, and try to get the window seat, so that you will not be disturbed when your seatmates get up. You could also bring eye patches, which will mask the light inside the plane. (Credit for this idea goes to Sam Shank, CEO and co-founder at HotelTonight.)

If you do not plan to sleep on a flight, aim for aisle seats as much as possible. This allows you to get up and move more easily and

more often. As discussed in chapter 4, sitting puts 40–90 percent
more pressure on your lower back than standing, so it's wise to get
up often during plane rides.[14] You can also bring a bottle of water to
stay hydrated, and you can bring healthy snacks to help you re-fuel
in-flight.

Bring Fuel for Your Trip

In addition to bringing water and fuel for your time in transit, you
can also bring non-perishable fuel for the rest of your trip. As discussed in chapter 4, the following can come in handy during travel:

- Organic, grass-fed jerky
- Nuts or nut butters
- Roasted chickpeas
- Fresh fruit (firmer fruits like apples are best for travel)
- Oats
- Tuna packets
- Fish oil
- Greens supplement
- Multi-vitamin
- Vitamin D
- Unflavored whey protein powder or vegan protein powder
- Magic Bullet blender

You could also pick up some healthy items after arriving at your
destination. This works well for perishable items that require no
prep time, like hard-boiled eggs or Greek yogurt.

Sweat During Your Trip

You will also feel better and perform better if you work out during your time away from home. For example, Mukesh Aghi, president at the U.S.-India Strategic Partnership Forum (USISPF), told
me that he always makes time for physical activity after lengthy
journeys, like the sixteen-hour ones that he takes between the
United States and India. "When I land, I go straight to the gym,
and work out for thirty to sixty minutes to get the blood flowing,"
he said.

Rhonda Vetere, CTO at Estée Lauder Companies, is a road warrior who also swears by this practice right after long flights. "It gives me more energy," she said. "When you travel, you have to be healthy, or you will get sick."

Some people, including Mukesh and Rhonda, actually work out *more* when they travel, since there are fewer non-work commitments when you are on the road. "My fitness intensity has actually increased as my travel schedule has increased through the years, and my workout schedule is actually more intense when I'm on the road than when at home," Rhonda told me.

Consider bringing a jump rope and some resistance bands in your luggage. They can come in handy if the equipment is limited at your hotel. You could also use exercise as a way to get out of your hotel and explore the local area and culture, either by going on your own walking/running tour of the area or by attending a local group exercise class.

Rhonda Vetere, chief technology officer at Estée Lauder Companies

Turn Your Hotel Room into a Sleep Sanctuary

Try to mirror the conditions that you prefer at home. For example, you could bring a sleeping mask (in case your room is not dark enough for you), a white noise machine (in case your hotel is noisy), and a travel pillow (in case your hotel's pillows are not your preferred thickness or firmness).

Bring Equipment to Create a Pain-Free Desk

As discussed in chapter 4, you could also bring a wireless keyboard and portable monitor stand, so that you can set up a pain-free laptop/desk from any remote location.

Despite all of your planning, some travel factors will still be out of your control. In addition to delays and last-minute cancelations, I have also had airlines lose my bags, including one time in Sweden when I was scheduled to compete in an obstacle race called "Toughest Ice" the next morning. You have probably had to deal with lost bags as well, although I hope such an experience never causes you to have to run five miles in the snow while wearing replacement cleats that are three sizes too small.

CHAPTER SUMMARY

You can try to multitask or you can focus. You cannot do both. This chapter featured tips on maximizing travel, along with three stronger work habits to achieve more in much less time:

- Stronger work habit #1: Focus on one task at a time
- Stronger work habit #2: Plan your day in advance
- Stronger work habit #3: Work like an athlete

Remember *the Headlights Method*. For example, if you typically try to multitask, it would likely be unrealistic and overwhelming to immediately start trying to focus on one task at a time for the entire day. So, maybe you could initially try to focus on one task at a time for the first thirty or sixty minutes of each workday. Expand the habit or add on the next one whenever you are ready. Here are some questions that you might want to ask yourself as you reflect on this chapter:

- How do you feel and perform when you focus on one task at a time? How do you feel and perform when you try to multi task?
- What are your greatest obstacles in regard to your work habits? How could you overcome these obstacles?
- How could you incorporate *Boost Breaks* into your workdays?

CHAPTER 9

RENEW

You should sit in meditation for twenty minutes every day,
unless you're too busy. Then you should sit for an hour.

—Zen proverb

How do you think you would perform at work if you drank enough beer, wine, or liquor throughout each day to maintain a blood alcohol level that approached or exceeded the legal limit? Deprive yourself of enough quality sleep, and you will find out. A study by researchers in Australia found that sleep deprivation can reduce performance as much as being impaired or legally intoxicated from drinking too much alcohol.[1]

There are many myths about sleep and personal renewal. Here are three of the most common:

- Myth #1: You can increase your productivity by cutting back on your sleep.
- Myth #2: Personal renewal is just for people who want to have "more balance."
- Myth #3: You have to be a "morning person" to be productive in the morning.

In this chapter, we'll tackle each of these fallacies, and others. All of your time outside of work (before work, after work, and during your weekends) has a profound impact on your energy, stress, and performance at work. You will learn three personal renewal habits that will help you feel and perform your best each day and each week. Let's start with that first myth.

BETTER SLEEP = BETTER PERFORMANCE

Poor sleep reduces your brainpower, decreases your energy, makes you more irritable and anxious, weakens your immune system, hinders your muscle growth and recovery, and leads to weight gain. Getting quality sleep is not a waste of time. It's actually one of the best uses of your time if you want to look, feel, and perform your best.

Nonetheless, many people believe they can increase their productivity by cutting back on their sleep. This is a common side effect of buying into the myth that the longer you work, the better. "A recurring theme I hear from entrepreneurs is how little they sleep," said Jeff Stibel, a brain scientist, entrepreneur, and co-founder (with Kobe Bryant) of Bryant Stibel, a venture capital fund. "They rationalize that the less they sleep, the more productive they are.

"As a brain scientist, this is a pretty appalling thought. Lack of sleep is linked to underperformance, not overachievement. From chronic fatigue to confusion, poor decision-making, irritability, headaches, weight gain, depression, heart disease; the list goes on and on. None of us are immune to a lack of sleep, no matter how busy or important you are."

Other brain health experts agree. "Many people think of sleep as this period when they aren't doing anything, but nothing could be further from the truth," said Dr. Daniel Johnston, co-founder at BrainSpan, a brain health analytics company. "There are many physiological processes taking place in your brain and your body when you sleep. You should think about your seven to eight hours of sleep like 'going to the gym for your brain' for seven to eight hours."

Sleep duration is not the only factor to monitor, however. Quality matters as well. "People staying up late drinking alcohol or taking sleeping aids might be asleep for what seems like a good amount of time, but they aren't getting enough *quality* sleep," said Dr. Johnston.

What about those who claim that sleeping less than six hours a night is a key to their success? Well, many of these people eventually realize their "Success Delusion" and recognize that their sleeping habits actually held them back, rather than helped them reach their full potential.[2] Just ask former US President Bill Clinton, a man known for sleeping less than six hours a night during much of his career. Clinton later said, "Every important mistake I've made in my life, I've made because I was too tired."[3]

STRONGER RENEWAL HABIT #1: END YOUR DAY STRONG

While some people buy into the myth that you increase productivity by cutting back on sleep, many high performers recognize that proper sleep is essential to feeling and performing your best. One such example is Dr. Josh Riff, CEO at Onduo. "Getting enough sleep is the best investment that you can make," Josh told me. "As I've gotten older and wiser, I'm willing to skip a workout occasionally in order to get more sleep. I know it will help me at work the next day and help me be stronger when I exercise again. Ideally, you want to follow a schedule and have a bedtime ritual."

A well-designed bedtime routine will dramatically improve your sleep and your overall health, well-being, and performance. It can also make the next morning/day easier and be used as a time to bond with people that you care about. Ideally, you want to start winding down thirty to sixty minutes before bed.

According to integrative neurologist Dr. Kulreet Chaudhary, there are benefits to getting to bed by 10:00 p.m. "The deepest and most regenerative sleep occurs between 10 p.m.–2 a.m.," she said. "If your body is chronically deprived of the regenerative sleep between 10 p.m.–2 a.m., then you may still feel fatigued when you wake up in the morning."[4]

In addition to timing, here are some more ideas on how to end your day strong with a better bedtime routine:

Spend Quality Time with Family

When my brother Matt and I were little kids, my mother and father would tell us stories before sleep. Decades later, we all smile when remembering the stories of superheroes, cartoon characters, and the various actors of my parents' imagination.

If you have a significant other and/or children, what about ending the day together in a special way? For example, Sam Shank, co-founder and CEO at HotelTonight, told me that one of his sons has trouble falling asleep. "We often spend time together doing deep breathing before bed," Sam said. "It's been really good for him and it helps me go to bed too."

Read

In one study, researchers at the University of Sussex found that reading for as little as six minutes could reduce stress levels by up to 68 percent.[5] Mukesh Aghi, president at the U.S.-India Strategic Partnership Forum (USISPF), has read at night since graduate school, completing one to two books each week, on average. "I don't watch any TV for a few hours before bed," he told me. "I shift to listening to music and reading. This takes the edge off the day."

If you choose to read before bed, give some thought to *how* you read. As discussed in chapter 4, studies have found that reading on a device can dramatically reduce sleep quality.[6] This makes a big difference for many people, including Jennifer Carr-Smith, a SVP at Groupon. "I don't read on a Kindle or iPad before bed," she said. "That's not relaxing because technology symbolizes work to me. I prefer to read physical books before sleep."

Be mindful about *what* you read as well. Many people find non-fiction business books or political content to be too stimulating at the end of the day. At night, you might want to stick to fiction or light non-fiction.

Journal

You may have heard of the concept of a "gratitude journal." Research has demonstrated that doing one before bedtime can improve sleep quality. In one experiment, scientists at the University of Manchester in England studied a group of people of all ages (40 percent of whom had sleep disorders). They found that gratitude was associated with falling asleep faster and with having greater sleep quality.[7]

If you would like to journal, I recommend that you take it one step further, though, and do what I refer to as a *Power Journal*. With this approach, you write down at least three things each night that you are thankful for from the day, and you also write down three things each night *that you are proud of doing that day*. Think of the long-term impact that keeping a *Power Journal* could have on your life. Give thanks for three things a day, and you will take time to appreciate more than one thousand positive elements in a year. Record three actions a day that you are proud of, and you will take and acknowledge over one thousand confidence-building, progress-making steps in a year.

By becoming more mindful of everything good in your life, you will start to notice *and search for* things to be grateful for, many of which you might currently be missing or taking for granted. By recognizing what you are proud of each day, you will also start to notice *and search for* opportunities to move toward your goals, to step out of your comfort zone, and to add value to the world. You will also take time to celebrate your effort.

How Else Can You End Your Day Strong?

There are many other elements that you could include in your bedtime routine. You could listen to peaceful music, you could go for a walk, you could take a bath, you could perform some light stretching or yoga, or you could meditate. Each of these activities is linked to lower stress and better sleep. You could also complete a few tasks that would otherwise have to occur when you wake up. This makes for an easier morning.

Equally important is what you do not do late at night. Before bed, avoid anything that is stimulating (like electronics or caffeine) or that can throw off your sleep (like alcohol). The National Sleep Foundation also recommends not eating large meals within the two to three hours before bed.[8]

Serial entrepreneur Alex Douzet told me that he tracked his sleep and found that he slept better and deeper when he cut out processed foods. Studies have proven this as well. In one experiment by Columbia University, researchers found that high sugar intake and low fiber intake (what you usually find in processed foods) was associated with poorer sleep quality.[9] If you usually have trouble falling asleep, or if you wake up frequently in the middle of the night, your eating habits could be what's causing the problem.

Track Your Sleep

Thanks to health and fitness trackers and sleeping apps like Sleep Cycle, you can conduct your own self-experiments to figure out which environmental conditions and pre-sleep activities work best for you. You can also analyze how you feel and perform when you go to bed at certain times and after getting certain amounts of sleep. The National Sleep Foundation recommends seven to nine hours each night for most adults.[10] Experiment to see what works best for you.

What if you have a partner with different sleeping habits or preferences?

Well, you could consider sleeping in separate rooms or in separate beds, either every night or on certain nights. While this might sound strange, one poll by The National Sleep Foundation found that 25 percent of couples sleep separately.[11] Other surveys have reported even higher percentages.

> **Work Stronger Wisdom**
> "You could take away anything else, but do not take away my sleep."
>
> —Barbara Tulipane, CEO at National Recreation and Park Association (NRPA)

STRONGER RENEWAL HABIT #2: START YOUR DAY STRONG

Imagine that it is 8:17 a.m. on a Tuesday morning. After hitting the snooze button for the fifth time, you decide it is finally time to get up. You have to be at work by 9:00 a.m. Your commute takes about thirty minutes, so you will probably be late unless you are out of the house in the next thirteen minutes. You head to your bathroom, turn on the shower, and jump in immediately. You frantically scrub on and rinse off some soap. Then, you turn off the shower, towel off rapidly, and walk to your closet. It is now 8:20 a.m.

You did not prepare your work outfit the night before, so you search around until settling on several pieces of clothing that appear the least wrinkled. There is no time for ironing. After getting changed, you brush your teeth for seven seconds. Then, you run downstairs and head out the door. You do not have time for breakfast. It is now 8:24 a.m.

You begin a power-walk (actually, it's more like a jog) to the train station. You arrive at 8:29 a.m. Luckily, the trains are moving quickly that day and you get to your stop at 8:53 a.m. You get off the train and go back to a light jog. You arrive at work with three minutes to spare, but you are a little sweaty and your heart is racing.

Not exactly a peaceful way to start the day, huh?

Unfortunately, this was a typical morning for me right after college. Each day, I abused the snooze button on my alarm clock and slept way too late. Then I scrambled like a lunatic to get to work on time.

The pace and flow of your morning sets the tone for the rest of your day. Start your day frazzled, and you will carry that stress with you for hours. Start your day strong, and the rest of the day will be easier. A great morning routine nourishes your body, mind, and spirit and helps you show up at work as your best possible self.

Mornings are a great time for important activities that might be difficult to complete later in the day. As Laura Vanderkam writes in *What the Most Successful People Do Before Breakfast*, "Seizing your mornings is the equivalent of that sound financial advice to pay yourself before you pay your bills. If you wait until the end of the month to save what you have left, there will be nothing left over. Likewise, if you wait until the end of the day to do meaningful but not urgent things like exercise, pray, read, ponder how to advance your career or grow your organization, or truly give your family your best, it probably won't happen."[12]

The most successful people *dominate* their mornings. While the individual preferences can vary significantly, this theme came up over and over during my research for this book.

Exercise is one way to start your day strong. For example, Jennifer Carr-Smith, a SVP at Groupon, told me that she likes to work out when she wakes up. "If I don't exercise in the morning, it doesn't happen later on," she said. This sentiment is common, especially when you are juggling a demanding career and a family, as Jennifer is as an executive, wife, and mother of three children.

You can also use time before work to bond with your family. Personal and professional conflicts are much less likely to surface at 6:30 a.m. than at 6:30 p.m. What about having family breakfasts in addition to or instead of family dinners? After her morning workout, Jennifer typically eats breakfast with her husband and their three children.

You can also use part of your mornings to reflect and be mindful. For example, Tara-Nicholle Nelson, founder and CEO at Transformational Consumer Insights, told me that she starts her day by journaling with "morning pages," a habit that she learned about by reading *The Artist's Way: A Spiritual Path to Higher Creativity* by Julia Cameron. "If someone said I could only do one well-being practice in my life, I would choose 'morning pages,' even over working out, which is also very important to me," said Tara-Nicholle. "This is the first thing that I do every morning. It's like my 'emotional windshield wipers.' This is also where I go to solve my toughest problems."

Tony Robbins, a #1 *New York Times* best-selling author, entrepreneur, and philanthropist, also includes mindfulness in his morning routine. He has a unique way of starting his day before that, though. In 2016, he shared his ritual with Thrive Global. The very first thing that he does when he wakes up is jump into ice cold water. It is not something he wants to do. He does it "both as a mental discipline, and also because it stimulates the blood flow of the lymph nodes and the body. You feel fully alive," he said.[13]

After his "cold plunge," he then invests at least ten minutes in something he refers to as "priming." First, he focuses on three moments in his life for which he is grateful. Then he does a three-minute blessing and prayer for his own body's health and for all the people in his life. Then he concentrates on his "three to thrive," where he focuses on three outcomes he wants to accomplish. "I see them, and feel them, and experience them as done, and I feel grateful for them," he said.[14]

What If You Are Not a Morning Person?

If you do not feel great when you wake up—physically, mentally, or psychologically—you could use that as a cue to initiate a routine designed to make you feel better. You do not need to be a "morning person" to start your day strong. You could decide that you will take control of your mornings *because* you are not a morning person. Either way, if you think that you are "not a morning person," beware of this fixed mindset belief (see chapter 2).

These days, a highly choreographed morning routine transforms me naturally into a radically different, much stronger human being. My alarm generally goes off between 5:00 a.m. and 6:00 a.m. (at a time decided the night before). I get up right away. No more snoozing. Then I make my bed, fuel up, brush my teeth, get changed into workout clothes, and head to an exercise venue for a focused workout. After returning home, I re-fuel, shower, get changed for work, and head out the door ready to tackle the world. It is impossible to quantify the impact that a stronger morning routine has had on my life.

Wyatt Everhart, an Emmy Award–winning meteorologist, also takes control of his mornings, even though this does not come naturally to him either. "There are many days that I wake up and don't feel that great since I don't consider myself to be a morning person," he told me. "However, after a hard workout, I almost always feel great, and I always have more overall energy throughout the day."

How Else Can You Start Your Day Strong?

As a point of emphasis, you do not have to begin your day by exercising intensely, by journaling about your emotions, or by plunging into forty-degree water. There are many other things that you could do before work to set a positive tone for your day. This includes activities that also work well before bed, such as listening to music, going for a walk, stretching, doing yoga, or meditating. You could also use some of your morning time for a personal hobby that energizes you.

The key message is to take control of your mornings, instead of allowing your mornings to control you.

Refuse to Snooze

If you usually snooze in the morning and you want to break this habit, there are a few ways that you could do it. In addition to turning your bedroom into a better sleeping environment and developing a better bedtime routine, you could also go to bed earlier. Each of these steps would likely remove or reduce a common cue (fatigue) that can trigger your snoozing habit. Keeping your alarm clock at least ten feet away from your bed would also make it harder to snooze.

Finally, you could develop an exciting morning routine and focus on the meaningful goals and relationships in your life. This is one way that Sam Shank, co-founder and CEO at HotelTonight, turned himself into an early-riser, even though he does not consider himself a morning person either. "It's so much easier to get out of bed when you have a sense of purpose and are excited about the day ahead," he wrote. "I get energized thinking about the meetings on my calendar, the incredible people I get to work and brainstorm and solve big problems with, and the time I spend with my family."[15]

Reboot Your Commute

A miserable commute can reduce or erase the benefits of an otherwise energizing morning routine. According to the Department of Transportation, the average person spends about two hundred hours traveling to and from work each year.[16] Instead of allowing your daily transit to be a source of stress and irritation, are there some ways that you can take control of this experience and turn it into a source of leisure, relaxation, or productivity?

First of all, give yourself a cushion so that you won't be late, even when you face unexpected delays. You can also consider different modes of transportation. Depending on where you live and work, you may be able to commute by car, by train, by bus, by boat, by foot, by bike, or by a combination. Or, if you have several hundred thousand dollars to burn, you could commute by private jet, as former California Governor Arnold Schwarzenegger apparently used to do.[17] If you have no choice but to travel via a crowded form of public transportation, give some thought to how you could make the experience more enjoyable. If you want to relax and disconnect, maybe you could listen to music and/or focus on deep breathing. Or, maybe you would prefer to use this time for another hobby or activity that is possible during transit. For example, one of my co-workers uses his bus commutes to edit videos of his son's basketball games. As another example, one of my friends uses his train rides to read more than twenty books each year.

Even if your commute is very uncomfortable or long, there is always someone who has it worse. An article in the *Daily Mail* featured a man in Britain who commutes 183 miles *each way* to and from his office every day. That's nearly 100,000 miles a year and similar to driving from New York City to Baltimore every morning and back to New York City each night![18]

STRONGER RENEWAL HABIT #3: END YOUR WEEK STRONG

There are sixty-four hours between 5:00 p.m. on Friday and 9:00 a.m. on Monday. If you sleep eight hours on Friday, Saturday, and Sunday night, you still have forty hours between work weeks. That is an enormous amount of time (over 2,000 hours each year) that can be wasted away or invested wisely in activities and people that are important to you.

The best weekends energize you for the week ahead and usually include a combination of quality time with friends and family, leisure, physical activity, and personal and professional growth. The best weekends, like the best trips, do not just happen though. They require advanced planning.

There are two major problems with waiting until the last minute to decide how to use part or all of your weekend. First of all, you eliminate the satisfaction that comes from anticipation. Why do most people book vacations months in advance? This is largely to be able to look forward to them before experiencing them. The second reason to plan ahead is more practical. If you want to include other people in your weekends, you need to give them notice. This was not required earlier in life.

While in college, my roommates and I often hosted large parties that we organized at the last minute. When we were in the mood, we would call or text our friends after dinner. Next thing we knew, there would be at least twenty-five to fifty people at our place. This might have been partly due to the fact that we went to Johns Hopkins University, a college that was once ranked among the worst party schools in the country. We were often the only game in town.

When you're an adult, many of the people who you want to spend time with will have families and various commitments that will prevent them from being as spontaneous as they could be earlier in life. For example, two of the friends that I hosted those college parties with are each married now, and they each have kids. The only way that we can get together these days is when we schedule it weeks or months in advance.

You do not need to script every second of your weekends ahead of time. You can simply identify a few weekend activities in advance. Again, by doing so, you get to look forward to them. There are countless ways to design your weekends. Here are some ideas:

Focus on Friends and Family

You can start with meaningful activities with your favorite people. Even just a few hours of focused attention will do much more for your relationships than a much longer period of time in which you try to multitask and are distracted by social media or emails. Yes, this is incredibly obvious advice, but it is worth emphasizing. How often do you see families or groups of friends buried in their cell phones, instead of enjoying each other's company?

> **Work Stronger Wisdom**
> "When I am with my kids on a weekend, I am 100 percent focused on them during that time. I'm not on my phone or answering texts or emails from work."
>
> —Alex Douzet, serial entrepreneur

Combine Family Time and Exercise

You could also incorporate physical activity into your family time. "When my kids were younger, people would always ask how I found the time to train," said Ken Lubin, managing director at ZRG Partners and founder of Executive Athletes. "I would often take my kids with me and push the stroller for a fifteen- to twenty-mile run. The kids had fun, I got in a long workout and spent time with my kids, and my wife would have a few hours for herself."

Combine Exercise with Local Adventures

Weekend workouts can also be a fun way to explore new areas— either with others or on your own. While preparing for a big race, I once used eight straight Sundays to train at and explore various trails and parks within one to two hours of my home. Each weekend was a mini-adventure that I planned in advance and looked forward to all week long.

Combine Exercise and Brainstorming for Work

You could also combine physical activity with a brainstorming session for work. While multitasking is not effective on two separate mental tasks (see chapter 8), you can use your body and your mind at the same time, if you keep your intensity at a "low" or "moderate" level. That way, it is possible to think about something else simultaneously. For example, Juan Uro, an EVP at the NBA, told me that he has a lot of creative ideas during long runs on the weekends. "It's a great time to think without distraction," he said.

"Play Defense" and "Play Offense" for Your Career

While Saturdays and Sundays are clearly great times to disconnect from work, you could also carve out a few windows of time to focus on your career. You could "play defense" by catching up on emails or anything that slipped through the cracks during the week. This is like taking a shower after a long week of work leaves you sweaty. You could "play offense" by reviewing the last week and setting goals for what you want to accomplish during the upcoming week (as discussed in chapter 8).

Disconnect from Work

Even if you decide to do some work on the weekends, it is equally important to carve out time away from your career, even if only for one full day or part of one day. This will help you show up on Monday with a fresher perspective than if you work through the entire weekend. "I say no to things all the time because they are on Sundays," said Tara-Nicholle Nelson, founder and CEO at Transformational Consumer Insights. "Instead, I go to church or stream it if I'm traveling. I also just try to spend Sundays enjoying myself and with people I care about. I don't check emails on Sundays."

How Else Could You End Your Week Strong?

In addition to the ideas discussed above, you could participate in a meaningful community service project, read a great book, attend a religious/spiritual ceremony that is important to you, check out a new or favorite restaurant, cook a new or favorite recipe, visit a new or favorite park, go to a movie, take a class on a topic of interest, attend a comedy show, sporting event, or concert, or enjoy a hobby like writing, painting, or photography.

GO WITH THE FLOW

No discussion of personal renewal would be complete without emphasizing yoga, mindfulness, and meditation. A growing number of top performers are embracing these practices since they can strengthen your brain and provide a number of mental and psychological benefits, including lower stress and a greater ability to concentrate. For example, one study published in *Journal of Physical Activity & Health* found that yoga could be more effective than aerobic exercise in enhancing cognitive performance.[19] Yoga also provides a number of physical benefits, including improved sleep quality, lower blood pressure, greater flexibility, better posture, better balance, and stronger joints, bones, and muscles.[20]

Steven Sinofsky (an investor, board member, and former Microsoft executive) told me that he tries to practice yoga almost every day for sixty to ninety minutes. He often practices with his eyes closed as a way to change it up. "Because yoga is a 'moving meditation,' I like to think of this as my personal disconnect time," he said. "Most studios don't permit phones and it really works. As soon as you walk in, you get focused on your mat. That hour when you are getting something done, while being disconnected, is special because it doesn't feel like I'm forcing myself to be disconnected."

Janine Allis, founder of Boost Juice, told me that she took up yoga when she was forty years old and could not touch her toes. "I had basically spent the last ten years sitting in chairs and on airplanes," she said. "Yoga had to break my body down before it could be put back together again. My body is so much stronger now [at fifty-one years old]. I can do things now that I couldn't even do when I was twenty. I am also calmer and things don't rattle me like they used to. Yoga has been quite transformative for me."

Janine Allis, founder of Boost Juice

As our world becomes more and more turbulent, even those who were previously skeptical are embracing these practices. One such person is Scott O'Neil, CEO at Harris Blitzer Sports & Entertainment. "These days, I get up at 5:30 a.m. and do a ten-minute, faith-based devotional. Then, I meditate," Scott told me. "If you had told me ten years ago to meditate, I would have laughed. It probably would have been the best thing for me, but I wasn't ready for it then.

I am a big advocate for meditation and mindfulness now though. It helps me be more focused and feel more alive.

"My wife and I have three daughters. Our home is full of love and energy, but chaos. The peacefulness I find in the morning through these rituals is something that I do not experience later in the chaotic day. This quiet time is a great way to center and ground myself," Scott said.

Yoga, mindfulness, or meditation can work with any schedule. You could hook these practices onto your morning routine, your lunch break, your bedtime routine, or a weekend activity. Even five to ten minutes a day can lead to more energy, less stress, and greater focus.

What Is Meditation and Mindfulness?

According to Headspace, a popular digital service that provides guided meditation sessions and mindfulness training, mindfulness is defined as "the intention to be present in the here and now, fully engaged in whatever is happening, free from distraction or judgment, with a soft and open mind." Headspace defines meditation as "the simple exercise to familiarize oneself with the qualities of mindfulness."[21]

CHAPTER SUMMARY

Quality sleep and personal renewal are fundamental to feeling and performing your best. This chapter highlighted three habits outside of work to help you be your best each day and each week:

- Stronger renewal habit #1: End your day strong
- Stronger renewal habit #2: Start your day strong
- Stronger renewal habit #3: End your week strong

Remember *the Headlights Method*. For example, if revamping your entire bedtime routine (habit #1) feels overwhelming, you could start by focusing only on one component, like reading, journaling, or meditating each night before bed. Expand the habit (and/or add on the next one) whenever you are ready. Here are some questions that you might want to ask yourself as you reflect on this chapter:

- How do you feel and perform when you are well-rested? How do you feel and perform when you are not well-rested?
- What could you stop doing or start doing before bed to improve your sleep quality?
- What could you stop doing or start doing before work to take more control of your mornings?

CHAPTER 10

STRONGER COMPANIES

Take care of your employees, and they'll take care of your business. It's as simple as that.
—Sir Richard Branson, founder of Virgin Group

I once spoke with a member of the executive team for a multi-billion-dollar company with over five thousand employees. We discussed how this woman keeps herself healthy. We also talked about what her company has done to enhance the well-being of its people.

When asked about her organization, she told me about a program that helped several hundred employees discover they were at high risk for a number of potentially life-threatening illnesses. I then asked what her company did for the rest of the organization, which included more than 90 percent of their workforce.

"You are on to something," she replied. "We haven't really taken that approach though. I guess we have basically just focused on those who are the unhealthiest."

There are many myths about wellness in the workplace. Here are three of the most common:

- Myth #1: Wellness programs are only for your unhealthiest employees.
- Myth #2: Artificial incentives are the best way to motivate your employees.

- Myth #3: Wellness programs only need to focus on physical activity.

In this chapter, we'll tackle each of these fallacies, and others. One size or approach does not fit all when it comes to creating a stronger company. An organization with 117 employees at one location faces vastly different challenges than a global organization with 117,000 employees. However, this chapter provides a six-step framework that any employer could use to reduce healthcare costs and to enhance health, well-being, and performance *for all employees.*

STRONGER EMPLOYEES = STRONGER COMPANY

Researchers at Duke Medicine have found that there is a direct relationship between an employee's weight and their medical care and pharmacy expenses. On average, healthcare costs are typically at least $1,000–$2,000 more each year for an overweight/obese worker than for someone of normal weight.[1] If your employee base is representative of the US population (where over 70 percent of people are overweight or obese[2]), that means your workforce's extra weight is likely costing you at least $700,000 to $1.4 million *for every 1,000 people that you employ.*

While significant, this data point is actually tiny in comparison to what your organization is likely losing due to absenteeism and presenteeism. Absenteeism is when employees miss work due to illness or other medical conditions, while presenteeism refers to when employees show up at work, but are unable to perform their best due to poor health.

Gallup has estimated that unhealthy employees in the United States miss 450 million more days of work each year than their healthier counterparts. This costs US employers an estimated $153 billion in lost productivity annually.[3] Even more astounding, Virgin Pulse (part of Sir Richard Branson's Virgin Group) has estimated that the costs of presenteeism are far greater—*more than ten times greater*—than the costs of absenteeism.[4]

These problems are not limited to the United States. They extend globally: obesity rates doubled in more than seventy countries between 1980 and 2017.[5]

While your organization should look for ways to reduce healthcare costs, it is a huge mistake to stop there. Unfortunately, many companies create wellness programs that focus exclusively on people who are the unhealthiest. Such programs are irrelevant to the majority of your workforce. They can also feel hollow to all employees, since they can give the impression that your organization only wants to save money. A more holistic approach will engage everyone, increase participation, and make it clear that your objectives are not strictly financial.

In a meta-analysis of the costs and savings associated with workplace wellness programs, Harvard researchers Katherine Baicker, David Cutler, and Zirui Song found that medical costs fall by about $3.27 for every dollar invested in wellness programs, and costs related to absenteeism fall by about $2.73 for every dollar invested.[6] While this research indicates a total return on investment (ROI) of six to one, a number of leaders are confident the true ROI is actually higher. One such leader is Robin Thurston, CEO at Helix, a consumer genomics company. "I believe that every dollar invested in employee well-being is worth at least ten dollars in productivity," he told me.

Put the numbers aside though. Isn't it logical to believe that there is a direct relationship between employee well-being and employee output? The stronger your people are—physically, mentally, and psychologically—the stronger your company will be, and the greater the impact that your organization can have on the world.

STEP #1: START AT THE TOP

I once attended a training seminar delivered by an independent consultant named Ted. My employer at the time hired him to run the program for our sales department. On the first day, Ted was introduced quickly by the leader of our group, a man named Nick. After introducing Ted, Nick stuck around for a few minutes. Then Nick disappeared for the rest of the day.

Nick's absence was a hot topic at lunch amongst the sales staff. The group speculated about all the possible reasons why he chose not to attend the program. A few people believed that he felt threatened by Ted, and that he was worried that he might be put on the spot during the training. A few others were convinced that he wanted some time for uninterrupted work. Another theory was that he simply did not see the value in the training and that *his* boss had mandated our department go through it.

Regardless of Nick's real reason for not being there, his decision had a very powerful impact. Some employees zoned out from the start, convinced that it must be a waste of their time. Nick's absence also impacted those of us who saw the value in the training. Since Nick had no idea what was covered, there was no way for him to reinforce what we learned. As a result, very little was retained.

Later in my career, I attended another internal training session. This program was not any better than the one that Nick blew off. However, the results of this program were far greater. This time, our leader (a man named Sam) took part in the entire session.

Like Nick's absence, Sam's presence also became a popular discussion topic. Several of us discussed how much we appreciated his attendance, along with his active participation. We all agreed that his actions during that day—more than any of his words before or after—made it quite clear that the program was important. In the months that followed, he also reinforced what we all had learned.

Leadership's absence (or presence) speaks louder than its words. Regardless of how you want to make your organization stronger, your leadership needs to buy in first and lead by example.

As Dr. Larry Senn and Jim Hart write in *Winning Teams Winning Cultures*, "All too often leaders in an organization approve of training programs dealing with issues such as leadership development or culture shaping, but don't attend them as participants or visibly work on the concepts themselves...We have found that the fastest way to create a positive self-fulfilling prophecy about cultural change is to have the top leaders individually and collectively shift their own behaviors. They don't have to be perfect, they just have to deal themselves into the same game they are asking others to play."[7]

> **Work Stronger Wisdom**
>
> "I believe there is real quantifiable business benefit to creating a culture focused on health and well-being. People who are healthier are going to be more productive, and they will be more engaged at work."
>
> —Chip Bergh, president and CEO at
> Levi Strauss & Co.

STEP #2: MOTIVATE EMPLOYEES NATURALLY (DON'T BRIBE, THREATEN, OR PUNISH)

In *Telling Ain't Training* by Harold Stolovitch and Erica Keeps, the authors share the following analogy to illustrate how people learn: "Imagine the following scene. In one hand I have a pitcher filled with water. In the other I have a glass with a lid. What happens when I try to pour water into the glass? Obviously, it spills over the glass and my hand because the inside is closed off."[8]

The authors then explain that this physical example is analogous to trying to pour your ideas into the closed mind of a learner.[9] In other words, learners (such as your employees) show up for any educational experience or change initiative with a "lid." Their lid includes their objections, self-limiting beliefs, doubts, and fears.

Your employees might not understand why change will be good for them (purpose). Even if your employees want to change, however, they might not be optimistic that they can. Their pessimism could be due to past failures. It could also be due to thinking they are "too busy" to change, thinking it's "too late" for them to change, or thinking that change will be "too difficult," take "too long," or be "too expensive."

> **Work Stronger Wisdom**
>
> "We focus on not just giving employees 'the what,' but also 'the why' and 'the how.'"
>
> —Dr. Joseph Callahan, director of Fitness
> Services at Phillips 66, a diversified
> energy manufacturing and logistics company

As a change agent, you must identify and remove the lid. You need to help employees understand why change is in their best interest, and you also need to help employees believe that change is possible. If you skip the essential step of removing the lid, change will not last, even if it somehow occurs in the short term. So, the obvious next question is: "How do you remove the lid?"

Don't Bribe, Threaten, or Punish

Before we discuss what to do, let's discuss what *not* to do. Some employers pay workers (or provide other extrinsic rewards) for logging a certain number of steps each day or for achieving other benchmarks deemed to be healthy. There is no doubt that the people and companies implementing these programs mean well.

Unfortunately, there are significant problems with this approach. When you incentivize people for doing something that they could want to do naturally, you ignore the reasons why they are not behaving in a healthier way in the first place. In other words, you try to pour water into a covered glass.

When you rely on artificial forms of motivation, you also perpetuate a myth that being healthy is a chore and something that you should only want to do if you get a prize. As Alfie Kohn writes in *Punished by Rewards: The Trouble with Gold Stars, Incentive Plans, A's, Praise and Other Bribes*, "Anything presented as a prerequisite for something else—that is as a means toward some other end—comes to be seen as less desirable. 'Do this and you'll get that' automatically devalues the 'this.' The recipient of the reward figures, 'If they have to bribe me to do this, it must be something I wouldn't want to do.'"[10]

To be clear, some studies have proven that financial incentives can lead to short term compliance and results. However, studies have also shown that incentives not only fail to produce long-term changes, but they can also encourage dishonest behavior, and do more harm in the long term.

In *Drive: The Surprising Truth About What Motivates Us*, author Daniel H. Pink also discusses the consequences of using contingent rewards. He highlights an extensive meta-analysis that was conducted in 1999. Dr. Edward L. Deci and two of his colleagues led this work and concluded the following: "Careful consideration of reward effects reported in 128 experiments lead to the conclusion that tangible rewards tend to have a substantially negative effect on intrinsic motivation."[11]

Want some additional evidence that contingent prizes are not effective? Consider that there are vendors who are profiting by running incentive programs for employers. In one such program that was highlighted on Fox Business Network, participants pay three hundred dollars to enter a weight loss challenge. If they achieve their goal, they receive one thousand dollars. If they fail, they lose their money.[12]

Where does their money go? It goes to the vendor running the challenge! Think about that. The vendor's profits actually increase as participant success decreases. The CEO of this vendor was asked by Fox Business Network about success rates in the program. He admitted that only 15–25 percent of people achieve their goal. His company has to pay those people, but his organization gets to keep the full entry fee from the 75–85 percent of people who fail.[13]

Motivate Employees Naturally

Emily Kolakowski, chief operating officer at Wellness Corporate Solutions (a company providing biometric screening services and comprehensive wellness programming), has some excellent recommendations on how to motivate employees naturally. Her company helps clients identify people in the organization who are interested in health and wellness and who can serve as internal wellness champions. "Then, we give these people the tools and resources to inspire and motivate their co-workers at their location," she told me. "We have also developed an online hub for wellness champions to collaborate inside the company and with other companies too.

"We also capture success stories on a monthly basis and we post them inside the online portal, so everyone can see. We want employees to think, 'Hey, if my co-worker can change, I can change too.'"

While Emily and her organization use different terminology ("wellness champions" and "success stories"), this strategy is similar to an optimism-boosting strategy covered in chapter 2—find a *Relevant Role Model*.

You can also increase employee motivation by hiring a nutritionist, fitness trainer, or wellness coach to meet with employees and help them address their wellness challenges privately. You could hire one or more experts on a part-time basis, or you could take it one step further, like The Motley Fool, a financial services company headquartered in Northern Virginia.

"In 2011, we hired our first full-time personal trainer at The Motley Fool. I wish we'd done so fifteen years sooner," wrote Tom Gardner, CEO and co-founder of the company. "Today, Samantha Whiteside [the company's chief wellness officer] presides over yoga, HIIT workouts, Zumba, and strength classes in spaces across our office. She coaches our colleagues around the world via Skype. The net result is a convenient solution for our employees that yields higher productivity, lower health insurance costs, and greater levels of satisfaction. Hire a full or part-time physical trainer; you'll make back this investment quickly."[14]

Contingent rewards and punishments make your company weaker, not stronger. What is my response to employers who have seen a ROI from introducing these measures? Imagine what their ROI might be if they were not using them. As Alfie Kohn wrote in *Punished By Rewards*, "Promising a reward to someone who appears unmotivated—or demotivated—is like offering salt water to someone who is thirsty: it's not the solution; it's the problem."[15]

Work Stronger Wisdom

"We believe our people are our greatest asset and that it's good business to take care of them. This leads to higher productivity, creativity, and engagement, and also creates stronger loyalty to the organization."

—Jennifer Fisher, national managing director of well-being at Deloitte

STEP #3: CREATE A STRONGER ENVIRONMENT

As covered in chapter 4, our environment provides physical and social cues that influence what and how much we eat, how much we move, and how much we focus and renew during the day. Here are some recommendations on how to create a stronger environment, so that all of your employees can thrive:

Re-Design Your Office Kitchens

In *Work Rules!: Insights from Inside Google That Will Transform How You Live and Lead*, Laszlo Bock, former SVP of People Operations at Google, shares data from experiments that Google conducted to analyze employee eating habits. In one experiment with the company's Boulder, Colorado, office, calories consumed from candy dropped by 30 percent just by placing candy into opaque containers in self-service stations that contained snacks and drinks. This made the candy less visible than healthier alternatives like fruit and nuts.[16] This same change was then implemented in Google's New York office. Over the next seven weeks, employees at that location consumed over three million fewer calories at work than usual.[17]

Like Google, you can make your office healthier by making the "dangerous" items (see chapter 6) less visible and less accessible. Use glass containers and prime real estate to make healthier options more visible and more accessible. You could also replace fattening foods with items that are more nutritious. Here are five examples:

- Provide naturally flavored water or 100 percent coconut water as healthier options than soda and other sugary beverages.
- Provide organic oats, hard-boiled eggs, or organic, plain, nonfat Greek yogurt as healthier breakfast options than bagels, pastries, or cereals.
- Provide nuts or nut butters as healthier options than chips and salty snacks.
- Provide fresh fruit as a healthier option than candy and other sweets.
- Provide organic, grass-fed jerky or roasted chickpeas as healthier high-protein options than artificial protein/energy bars.

You do not have to be maniacal about it though. As Sam Shank, CEO and co-founder at HotelTonight, told me, "It doesn't all have to be apples and pears. It's more about avoiding the really bad stuff than it is about only including the really healthy stuff. If someone wants to eat gummy bears, they certainly can, but I don't think we should be providing them."

Create a Workout Area On-site

A growing number of companies are creating workout areas on-site. Dick Costolo, former CEO at Twitter, highlighted the benefits of this when he and I spoke. "The gym [at Twitter] was the place where everyone came together," he told me. "You would have salespeople with finance people, engineers, designers, data science people, and people in HR. It was great for everyone to be able to see each other in a non-work setting on the same level. It also helped people talk to me back in the office in a way that they might not have otherwise felt comfortable. Doing these grueling workouts together made us feel more connected in the work environment," he said.

You do not need to build a fancy fitness center in order to encourage physical activity though. You can promote fitness simply by having showers and locker rooms on-site, and by organizing a group exercise activity before work, during lunch, or after work. (Costolo told me that Twitter started with group runs after work, before eventually building their own gym and offering CrossFit and yoga classes on-site.)

Another option is to dedicate part of your office space for exercise—either by blocking out an area permanently, or during certain times. This is one way that GreatCall, a company headquartered in San Diego, encourages physical activity. "We created a big space in the middle of our office where we don't have any desks," said David Inns, the CEO at GreatCall and a regular participant in the classes. "This has become our fitness room. It's literally in the middle of the office."

The company takes it further by hiring personal trainers and yoga instructors to lead group classes for employees at lunch every day. Even better, David serves as a healthy role model by participating in those classes (like Dick Costolo did at Twitter).

In lieu of (or in addition to) creating a workout area on-site, you could also structure a deal with a local gym. Chip Bergh, president and CEO at Levi Strauss, told me that he had his purchasing team work a deal with the Bay Club, one of the more elite gyms near Levi Strauss's headquarters in San Francisco. "We subsidize the membership fee because I think it's good for employees to have some skin in the game," Chip told me. "We now have almost five hundred people [half of the workforce at headquarters] who are members, and the usage is pretty high. There were only about seventy people who were members before we worked out this deal. Many people have told me this is the best benefit we offer."

> **Work Stronger Wisdom**
>
> "It's easier for our employees to eat right, be fit, and have an active, healthy lifestyle. It's actually more difficult to *not* be healthy and active here. It's more about our environment than any rules or one-line statements."
>
> —Bahram Akradi, chairman, CEO, and founder
> of Life Time®, the Healthy Way
> of Life Company

Create a More Active, More Focused Work Environment

Scott O'Neil, CEO at Harris Blitzer Sports & Entertainment, told me that he implemented a "no phones" policy for meetings. "You put your phone to the side as soon as you enter the room, not just when the meeting begins," he said. "Of course, it's a much-maligned policy, but it certainly helps us be more connected to each other. Asking the person next to you about their weekend is much more important than checking Twitter or responding to an email that can wait an hour."

You could also turn sitting meetings into walking meetings. If your group is not that large, you could have your meeting on the go. If your group is larger, you could all go for a walk together, and then have your gathering at a fixed location. One of my former employers did the latter with our weekly staff meetings, which were held in a separate conference room across the street from our main office location. Our employees always enjoyed getting some fresh air during the day and having a change of scenery. A short walk during the day will also give your people more energy. As discussed in chapter 8, one study found that ten minutes of low-intensity activity could make participants feel more energized than consuming 50 mg of caffeine, the amount found in a typical can of soda.[18]

Create a Nap Room or Wellness Room

Unilever has a "wellness zone" to provide employees with "a space for mindfulness, meditation, rest and recovery." The "wellness zone" has four sections, including an area stocked with healthy snacks, a separate area where employees can connect with colleagues, a separate area for yoga and stretching, and a completely silent area for breaks and rest.[19]

Work Stronger Wisdom

"The paradigm of just working harder and longer does not work anymore. We need to create environments where the whole person can show up—physically, emotionally, mentally, and spiritually. The most successful organizations pay attention to and create environments that support each of these elements."

—Laurie Coe, managing director, Organizational
Consulting, at The Energy Project

STEP #4: ORGANIZE FUN EVENTS

"There will probably be some moments today when you will ask yourself, 'Why the heck am I doing this?'" I say to my co-workers, several of whom look a little freaked out about what lies ahead. "Well, you'll be proud of yourself for finishing, and you'll have some great stories to tell."

It's 10:50 a.m. on a Saturday. I'm with fourteen of my colleagues from Heidrick & Struggles. We are ninety miles from our Washington, D.C. office, and we are less than ten minutes away from starting

Savage Race, an obstacle course race that is between five and seven miles long.

We enter the starting corral with about one hundred other Savages running in the 11:00 a.m. wave. Matty T, Savage Race's official emcee, starts getting us hyped up. "When I say Savage, you say Race!" he yells.

"Savage!" he screams.

"Race!" we yell back.

"Savage!"

"Race!"

"Savage!"

"Race!"

A few seconds later, and we are off. About a half-mile in, we come to our first obstacle. We take turns climbing over a wall with some footholds. Then, we have a brief run before we reach the "Venus Guy Trap," the first of many obstacles featuring water or mud. Reality officially sets in for anyone who thought they might somehow be able to stay dry today.

After another mile or so and a few more obstacles, we come to the "Shriveled Richard" obstacle where you have to jump into a dumpster full of ice water. There is a board in the middle, so you have to fully submerge and swim underwater for a few seconds. Then, you pop up on the other side of the board and wade through ten more feet of icy water to climb out the other side. After one of my co-workers makes it through, he yells out, "Oh my god!" Our team links up on the other side of the obstacle, and we all let out a few shivers before moving onward.

Next we come to the "Great Wall," an eight-foot-high wall. I get down on a knee and make a foothold with my hands. One of my female teammates pushes off my hands but gets stuck on top of the wall. I hesitate, while wondering to myself if or how you are allowed to touch a female co-worker in this situation. She ends up making it over on her own. Once we are both on the other side, she looks at me and says, "If I get stuck again, just grab my butt next time and push." We both laugh out loud.

About one mile later, we come to "Sawtooth," Savage Race's take on monkey bars. One of my colleagues makes it to the other side and proudly exclaims, "Wow, I can't believe I did that!"

Twenty minutes later, we reach the "Mud N' Guts" obstacle, a one-hundred-foot crawl through a pit of mud that is conveniently placed under barbed wire, so you have to stay low. I remind our team of the number one rule for an obstacle that involves mud: "Keep your mouth closed at all times." By the end of the pit, my entire body is completely covered in brown sludge. I offer a hug to one of my colleagues who chose to skip this obstacle. She declines.

About one mile later, we reach Colossus, "the prized jewel of Savage Race." This two-part obstacle combines a massive quarter pipe ramp on one side (sixteen feet high) and a huge water slide on the other side. According to Savage Race CEO Sam Abbitt, it takes five people working five days and costs about $40,000 to build this one obstacle.

Me (back row, fifth from left) with a group of my colleagues from Heidrick & Struggles, after completing a Savage Race event in Maryland

The quarter pipe has ropes hanging down about halfway. Once I'm at the top with one of my teammates, we take turns helping our other teammates get up and over. One of my female colleagues runs up the wall and grabs the rope, but she doesn't have the upper body strength to pull herself any higher. Two of us up top grab her arms. We have a firm grip, but she looks absolutely terrified, as she dangles fifteen feet off the ground. We grab her legs and help her swing her body over the wall. She looks incredibly relieved and thanks us for our help. How could you possibly replicate this sort of trust-building situation in the office or even in a traditional race?

We slide down the other side of the obstacle and get thrust into a huge pool of water. Then, we link up as a team again, complete the last obstacle and cross the finish line together. Fifteen of us started, and fifteen of us finished. We celebrate with some hugs, high-fives, and a team photo.

The following week, there was a flurry of emails and chatter around the office. Everyone agreed it was one of the most memorable, enjoyable days we had since joining the company. This shared experience forever changed the way we viewed each other. Here are some suggestions on how you can organize fun events for your company:

Form Teams for Obstacle Course Races

As my company found, obstacle course races can help co-workers bond in a way that simply will not happen during a traditional race, like a 5K walk or run. If you are intimidated about doing one of these events, recognize that they are designed to accommodate people of all fitness levels. "Some people have a misconception that everyone at our events is a great athlete in excellent shape," said Sam Abbitt, CEO at Savage Race. "While we do have many people who fit that profile, there are a lot of everyday, normal, average Joes who run in our events too."

Form Teams for Charity Walks or Runs

You can and should offer a variety of fun events, so that you can engage all employees, including those who will not want to participate in an obstacle course race. Several weeks after Savage Race, my office also participated in a 5K charity walk to raise money for Cystic Fibrosis. That event was more appropriate for some of our older, less active employees, although many people from our Savage Race team did the charity walk, too.

Create Your Own Fun Events

You could also create your own fun events. Hootsuite (the leading social media dashboard) creates fun pot-luck-style events to bring employees together and encourage healthy nutrition.[20] As another example, Barbara Tulipane, CEO at National Recreation and Park Association (NRPA), told me that her organization hosts a Staff Olympics every year. "Some people have physical limitations and we are respectful of that," she said. "It's not too serious. It's a celebratory, fun event."

Here are ten excellent ideas for fun events (some of these were already mentioned), thanks to SnackNation, a healthy snack delivery service for offices:[21]

- Get a company team together for an obstacle race or a more traditional race.
- Get a company team together to fundraise and participate in a charity walk/run.
- Get a company team together for a rec sports league.
- Hire yoga instructors or group exercise instructors to teach classes on-site.
- Take a company field trip to a gym or yoga studio and attend a class there.
- Set up a thirty-day fitness challenge.
- Host an employee cook-off or a healthy potluck.
- Hire a chef to teach a healthy cooking class on-site.

- Hire speakers to deliver on-site seminars on various wellness topics.
- Ask employees to deliver presentations on wellness topics in which they have expertise.

How Do You Know Which Events Will Work Best for Your Company?

You will increase participation in whatever you offer by targeting your programs for your audience, your location, and the time of year. "Programs for younger companies in Silicon Valley should be very different from programs for companies with much older employee bases," said Sarah Kalamchi, a wellness consultant who currently works at AirBnB, a community marketplace for booking unique accommodations around the world.

What's the best way to figure out what people will participate in? Ask them! While this surely sounds obvious, many HR leaders and wellness professionals design elaborate programs that employees never wanted in the first place. Involve your employees in the decision-making process, and they will be much more likely to participate.

> **Work Stronger Wisdom**
> "What is most important is understanding your company's culture and identifying what employees really want."
> —Jonathan Edelheit, president of Global
> Healthcare Resources and chairman of the
> Corporate Health & Wellness
> Association & Conference

Whatever is offered to employees, you want people to opt in voluntarily. Some people might prefer to be more private with their wellness journey. Make sure that you respect that. For example, one person at my office clearly didn't want to do Savage Race with us, but she reluctantly signed up because another co-worker kept bugging her about it. People who sign up under duress will likely back out last-minute, which is what eventually happened with her. Or, if they do participate, they might resent an experience that is supposed to be fun.

STEP #5: ENCOURAGE TOTAL WELLNESS

Wellness extends far beyond physical activity. Great employers focus on total wellness for all employees. Here are three examples that stood out from my research:

LinkedIn

The mission of LinkedIn's wellness program is "to assist employees in their pursuit of greatness." To achieve this inspiring objective, LinkedIn focuses on six key areas, which they refer to as "the Six Tenets of Wellness." This includes "Thoughts, Breathing, Hydration, Nutrition, Movement, and Rest."[22]

The company provides employees with a "Learning track" and an "Action track." The "Learning track" includes content that is delivered through an online portal and in-person presentations. The "Action track" consists of on-site activities (like fitness classes and speaker events), online offerings, and "in-community" opportunities for employees to practice wellness near their homes.[23]

LinkedIn employees also receive access to PerkUp!, an annual allowance that can be used for gym memberships, massages, and other wellness activities. "By including both learning and action, we believe that we create a robust and complete path that allows employees to incorporate the behaviors in their life that will drive the desired outcome," wrote Michael Susi, LinkedIn's wellness leader.[24]

Each month, LinkedIn also has one "Investment Day," or "InDay" for short. This tradition began in 2010 when the company had less than one thousand employees. By 2017, the workforce had grown to be more than ten times as large. Through this program, employees dedicate one day each month "to focus on themselves, the company, and the world."[25]

Deloitte

One of the world's premier professional services firms, Deloitte, also brings a holistic approach to this topic. Jennifer Fisher, national managing director of well-being at Deloitte, leads this area for the firm. "There's a persistent myth that well-being only entails physical health—medical and dental insurance, gym memberships and the like," she wrote. "But that's only one element; people have a number of needs. For instance, all the flextime in the world isn't going to help you feel engaged with your work if you don't have a sense of purpose. And without financial well-being, your emotional well-being may suffer."[26]

As one example of their complete approach to well-being, Deloitte has a unique paid family leave program, which they announced in September 2016. The program is sixteen weeks of paid leave for mothers and fathers welcoming a child from birth or adoption, and for employees that have a need to care for a sick family member—spouse, child, mother, father, brother, sister. "We want our people to know that we are there for them when they need us," Jennifer told me. "Some people may not ever need this leave, but just knowing that the organization has their back in this way has had a huge impact on our culture."

Basecamp

Formerly named 37signals, Basecamp is a private web application company based in Chicago, Illinois. The company was co-founded in 1999 and has more than 100,000 paying customers (as of 2017). In addition to offering very competitive financial benefits (including salaries in the top 5 percent in their industry and a 100 percent 401k match for up to 6 percent of salary), Basecamp strives to maximize employee health, well-being, and performance. As of January 1, 2017, the company offered the following employee benefits, among many others:[27]

- *To encourage healthier eating habits*: The company provides a "community supported agriculture (CSA) allowance," so that employees can have access to fresh, organic, local fruits and vegetables.
- *To encourage physical activity and movement*: The company provides a monthly fitness allowance ($100 per month). Employees can use this for gym/yoga memberships, race entries, or even new running shoes. The company also

provides standing desks for all employees, including those who work remotely.

- *To encourage greater focus and renewal*: The company encourages forty-hour work weeks, even though their industry often asks people to work over sixty hours a week. "In a crisis, or a once-every-couple-years special push, we may require very short-term extended hours, but otherwise we strongly encourage a maximum of forty hours a week, and eight hours of sleep a night," wrote Jason Fried, co-founder and CEO at Basecamp. The company also offers a monthly massage allowance ($100 per month), four-day work weeks in the summer, and employees are eligible for a one-month sabbatical every three years. In addition, Basecamp provides a $1,000 annual allowance for continuing education, and the company also matches donations to qualified charities (up to $2,000 per year per employee).

STEP #6: TRACK YOUR PROGRESS

As discussed in chapter 5, tracking progress increases your chances of achieving your goals, whatever they might be. According to *Working Well: A Global Survey of Workforce Well-being Strategies* (a survey conducted by Xerox in 2016), only 36 percent of respondents said they have measured specific outcomes from well-being programs globally.[28] It can be challenging to determine the ROI of programs intended to improve employee health, well-being, and productivity. However, you can monitor your progress by analyzing employee participation, employee engagement, and other key variables.

Laurie Coe, managing director, Organizational Consulting, at The Energy Project, told me that her firm starts by asking clients about the key business indicators that are causing them to question whether they are really getting the best out of their employees. "It could be high turnover, low engagement scores, burned out employees, or something else," she said. "Our consulting work is about uncovering why those results are occurring and then designing interventions to address the root causes. Ultimately our goal is to improve the engagement scores and to improve the employee experience that is contributing to the scores."

Laurie told me about one of her firm's clients that once received some very concerning data. While the client's employees were very engaged in their work, their people felt like they had no ability to balance work and family. "People were getting burned out, even though they loved their work. That really got their leader's attention," Laurie said.

The Energy Project consulted with the organization to determine how their employees could manage their energy differently in the face of all their commitments. When they re-surveyed the group a year later, the scores had improved significantly. "Not only did they have more balance, but ultimately they had more fulfilling lives. This was a crucial outcome for their leader," said Laurie.

While digital platforms can certainly enhance your programs and help you measure your success, technology is not without limitations. "There are some technology platforms that look incredible from the employer's side, but which are not built for users [employees]," said Jonathan Edelheit, president of Global Healthcare Resources and chairman of the Corporate Health & Wellness Association & Conference. "Bigger is not always better. Employers need to focus on engagement and utilization, not just which platform looks the best."

CHAPTER SUMMARY

The stronger your employees are—physically, mentally, and psychologically—the stronger your company will be. This chapter highlighted a six-step process to reduce healthcare costs and to maximize health, well-being, and performance for *all* of your people:

- Step #1: Start at the top
- Step #2: Motivate employees naturally (don't bribe, threaten, or punish)
- Step #3: Create a healthier environment
- Step #4: Organize fun events
- Step #5: Encourage total wellness
- Step #6: Track your progress

Here are some questions that you might want to ask yourself as you reflect on this chapter:

- What kind of example are your leaders currently setting for your employees? How could you encourage your leaders to serve as healthy role models?
- How could you motivate your employees naturally to make their health and well-being a priority?
- How could you create a healthier environment for your employees?

CONCLUSION

Self-conquest is the greatest of victories. Mighty is he who conquers himself.
        —Bruce Lee, martial artist, movie star, and cultural icon

I f you want to thrive now, and as you advance throughout your career, you need to *work stronger*, not longer. Stronger hours (not longer hours) are the key to feeling and performing your best over the long term.

Much of life is out of your hands. You cannot control the weather, the economy, or other people. However, *you have 100 percent control over your behavior.* You do not need anyone else's permission or approval to change the way that you work and live. While change is not easy, it's completely up to you, and it's never too late. You don't need a lot of time, you don't need gimmicks, and you don't need more willpower either.

Where there is a ~~will~~ why, there is a way. When change is difficult, remember why you started and why you should continue. Combine a desire to change (purpose), a belief that you can change (optimism), strategies for changing your behavior (the way), surroundings that support your desired behavior (environment), and strategies to hold yourself accountable (reinforcement), and you will have the P.O.W.E.R to accomplish anything.

Fuel yourself with stronger eating habits, sweat with stronger exercise habits, focus with stronger work habits, and renew with stronger personal renewal habits, and you will be amazed at how you can feel, what you can achieve, and how you can impact the world.

Let's end this book with a challenge: *I challenge you to make the next year (and every year after that) your strongest year ever.* You can achieve exceptional results over time by making changes that are simple and that might seem small. Stronger habits add up quickly. Incorporate one new behavior from this book into your life each month for the next twelve months, and you could transform your life (if you want to) over the next year.

I hope that this book has inspired you to expect and demand even more from yourself than you have in the past. You can be so much stronger than you realize. Take it one habit at a time.

—Pete Leibman

P.S. If you found this book helpful, I'd appreciate if you would recommend it to people who you think might benefit from it. They can grab their own copy and free bonuses at WorkStronger.com. Your support will help me share *Work Stronger* with a larger audience. Thanks for your help!

NOTES

INTRODUCTION

1   Marshall Goldsmith with Mark Reiter, *What Got You Here Won't Get You There: How Successful People Become Even More Successful* (New York: Hyperion, 2007), 16.

2   Ibid, 26.

3   "Being overweight 'ages people's brains,'" BBC News, August 4, 2016, http://www.bbc.com/news/health-36975089; Lisa Ronan et al., "Obesity associated with increased brain age from mid-life," *Neurobiology of Aging*, 2016, DOI: 10.1016/j. neurobiolaging.2016.07.010.

4   Stephen Willard, "Study: People Check Their Cell Phones Every Six Minutes, 150 Times A Day," Elite Daily, accessed on August 5, 2017, http://elitedaily.com/news/world/study-people-check-cell-phones-minutes-150-times-day/.

5   "The Myth Of Multitasking," NPR, May 10, 2013, http://www.npr.org/2013/05/10/182861382/the-myth-of-multitasking.

6   "How Sleep Loss Threatens Your Health," Harvard Health Publications, accessed on August 12, 2017, https://www.health.harvard.edu/healthbeat/how-sleep-loss-threatens-your-health.

7   David T. Neal et al., "Habits—A Repeat Performance," *Current Directions in Psychological Science* 15, no. 4 (2006): 198–202.

8   "Skittles," Wrigley, accessed on July 23, 2017, http://www.wrigley.com/global/brands/skittles.aspx#panel-3.

CHAPTER 1

1   Arianna Huffington, *Thrive: The Third Metric to Redefining Success and Creating a Life of Well-Being, Wisdom, and Wonder* (New York: Harmony Books, 2014), 1–2.

2   Ibid.

3   "About Thrive Global," Thrive Global, accessed on June 7, 2017, https://www.thriveglobal.com/about.

4   "Transformation in Just 12 Weeks," Gold's Gym, accessed on June 7, 2017, http://strength-exchange.goldsgym.com/2013/07/01/health-transformation-2/#michael.

5   Ibid.

6   Ibid.

7   Kate Devlin, "Healthy living 'cuts chronic disease by up to 80 per cent.'" *The Telegraph*, August 11, 2009, http://www.telegraph.co.uk/news/health/news/6005987/Healthy-living-cuts-chronic-disease-by-up-to-80-per-cent.html; Earl S. Ford et al., "Healthy Living Is the Best Revenge: Findings From the European Prospective Investigation Into Cancer and Nutrition-Potsdam Study," *Archives of Internal Medicine 169, no. 15* (2009): 1355–1362.

8   John J. Ratey, with Eric Hagerman, *Spark: The Revolutionary New Science of Exercise and the Brain* (New York: Little, Brown & Company, 2008), 122–123.

9   Andrew Lowndes, "Exercise reduces stress: UGA scientists discover why," University of Georgia, February 23, 2015, http://news.uga.edu/releases/article/galanin-stress-reducing-benefit/.

10 David Derbyshire, "A bowl of blueberries keeps the brain active in the afternoon," Dailymail.com, September 14, 2009, http://www.dailymail.co.uk/health/article-1212579/A-bowl-blueberries-day-keeps-brain-active-afternoon.html.

11 Jeffrey Kleim, "Exercise and the Brain," IDEA, March 1, 2011, http://www.ideafit.com/fitness-library/exercise-and-the-brain; S.J. Colcombe et al., "Aerobic exercise training increases brain volume in aging humans," *Journal of Gerontology*, Series A Biological Sciences and Medical Sciences 61, no. 11 (2006): 1166–70.

12 Heidi Godman, "Regular exercise changes the brain to improve memory, thinking skills," *Harvard Health Publications*, April 9, 2014, https://www.health.harvard.edu/blog/regular-exercise-changes-brain-improve-memory-thinking-skills-201404097111.

13 "the human era @ work; Findings from The Energy Project and Harvard Business Review," The Energy Project, accessed on August 11, 2017.

14 Joshua Gowin, "Brain Scans Show How Meditation Improves Mental Focus," *Psychology Today*, April 20, 2012, https://www.psychologytoday.com/blog/you-illuminated/201204/brain-scans-show-how-meditation-improves-mental-focus; Giuseppe Pagnoni, "Dynamical Properties of BOLD Activity from the Ventral Posteromedial Cortex Associated with Meditation and Attentional Skills," *Journal of Neuroscience 32, no. 15 (April 2012)*: 5242–9.

15 Michael Wilbon, "Kobe Bryant is feelin' all his years," ESPN, December 26, 2014, http://www.espn.com/nba/story/_/id/12079865/kobe-bryant-battle-father.

16 https://www.youtube.com/watch?v=nMzdAZ3TjCA

17 Karl Malone, "One Role Model to Another," *Sports Illustrated*, June 14, 1993, https://www.si.com/vault/1993/06/14/128740/one-role-model-to-another-whether-he-likes-it-or-not-charles-barkley-sets-an-example-that-many-will-follow.

CHAPTER 2

1 Walter Mischel. *The Marshmallow Test: Understanding Self-Control and How to Master It*, (London: Bantam Press, 2014), 70–73.

2 Ibid, 119–121.

3 Carol S. Dweck, *Mindset: The New Psychology of Success* (New York: Ballantine Books, 2006), 6.

4 Ibid, 7.

5 George Plimpton, Ed. *Writers At Work: The Paris Review Interviews* (New York: Penguin Books, 1977).

6   John Berardi, "The 3 Types of Clients," Precision Nutrition, accessed on August 23, 2017, http://www.precisionnutrition.com/how-to-coach.

7   "Mission & Vision," Mission & Vision, Back on My Feet, accessed on June 22, 2017, https://www.backonmyfeet.org/mission-vision.

CHAPTER 3

1   Brian Resnick, "The myth of self-control," *Vox*, November 24, 2016, https://www.vox.com/science-and-health/2016/11/3/13486940/self-control-psychology-myth.

2   Peyton Manning career stats, *Sports Reference*, accessed on July 17, 2017, https://www.pro-football-reference.com/players/M/MannPe00.htm.

3   Ibid.

4   Ryan Leaf career stats, NFL, accessed on July 17, 2017, http://www.nfl.com/player/ryanleaf/2501708/careerstats.

5   Erik Brady, Jim Corbett and Kimball Bennion, "Former quarterback Ryan Leaf's fall takes new turn," *USA Today*, accessed on July 17, 2017, http://usatoday30.usatoday.com/sports/story/2012-04-02/ryan-leaf-arrest-montana/53958116/1.

6   "Ryan Leaf Speaking Engagements," Transcend, accessed on July 17, 2017, https://transcendrecoverycommunity.com/ryan-leaf-speaking-engagements/.

7   Dan Fogarty, "This Is How Peyton Manning Prepares for a Big Game," SportsGrid, January 8, 2011, http://www.sportsgrid.com/real-sports/nfl/peyton-manning-preperation/.

8   Joe Thomson, "7 Most Interesting Busts in Draft History," the-Score, April 7, 2015, https://www.thescore.com/news/734961.

9   Kristin Hamlin, "Top 5 NFL Draft Disappointments: Why It's Better to Play with Your Heart," *Bleacher Report*, September 23, 2008, http://bleacherreport.com/articles/60728-top-5-nfl-draft-disappointments-why-its-better-to-play-with-your-heart.

10   Charles Duhigg, *The Power of Habit: Why We Do What We Do in Life and Business*, (New York: Random House Trade Paperbacks, 2014), 3.

11   Ibid, 19.

12   Ibid. 59.

13   Gretchen Rubin, *Better Than Before: Mastering the Habits of Our Everyday Lives*, (New York: Crown Publishers, 2015), 161; Wilhelm Hoffman et al., "Everyday Temptations: An Experience Sampling Study of Desire, Conflict, and Self-Control," *Journal of Personality and Social Psychology* 102, no. 6 (June 2012): 1318–35.

14   Brian Resnick, "The myth of self-control," *Vox*, November 24, 2016, https://www.vox.com/science-and-health/2016/11/3/13486940/self-control-psychology-myth; Wilhelm Hofmann et al., "Everyday temptations: an experience sampling study of desire, conflict, and self-control," *Journal of Personality and Social Psychology* 102, no. 6 (June 2012): 1318–35.

15   Walter Mischel. *The Marshmallow Test: Understanding Self-Control and How to Master It*, (London: Bantam Press, 2014), 134–136.

16   Ibid, 135.

17   Ibid, 256.

18   Brendon Burchard, *The Charge: Activating the 10 Human Drives That Make You Feel Alive* (New York: Free Press, 2012), 160–1.

19   Chip Heath and Dan Heath. *Switch: How to Change Things When Change Is Hard*, (New York: Broadway Books, 2010), 208; Todd F. Heatherton et al., "Personal Accounts of Successful Versus Failed Attempts at Life Change," *Personality and Social Psychology Bulletin* 20 (1994), 664–675.

20   Kristin Harmel, "Adding Variety To An Exercise Routine Helps Increase Adherence," University of Florida, October 24, 2000, http://news.ufl.edu/archive/2000/10/adding-variety-to-an-exercise-routine-helps-increase-adherence.html.

21   Dwayne Johnson (@therock), Instagram post, July 13, 2014, https://www.instagram.com/p/qaGrWRoh21/.

22   Stephen Galloway, "The Drive (and Despair) of The Rock: Dwayne Johnson on His Depression, Decision to Fire Agents and Paul Walker's Death," *The Hollywood Reporter*, June 8, 2014,

http://www.hollywoodreporter.com/features/drive-despair
-rock-dwayne-johnson-712689.

23   Mischel. *The Marshmallow Test*, 125–9; H.E. Hershfield et al.,
"Increasing Saving Behavior through Age-Progressed Render-
ings of the Future Self," *Journal of Marketing Research: Special
Issue* 48, SPL (2011): 23–37.

24   Mischel. *The Marshmallow Test*, 125–129; H.E. Hershfield
et al., "Increasing Saving Behavior through Age-Progressed
Renderings of the Future Self," 23–37.

25   Phillippa Lally et al., "How are habits formed: Modelling habit
formation in the real world," *European Journal of Social Psychology* 40 (2010): 998–1009, http://repositorio.ispa.pt/bit-
stream/10400.12/3364/1/IJSP_998-1009.pdf.

CHAPTER 4

1   Tony Robbins, "Tony Robbins: 'Gratitude Is the Solution to
Anger and Fear," Thrive Global, November 30, 2016, https://
journal.thriveglobal.com/tony-robbins-gratitude-is-the-solu-
tion-to-anger-and-fear-c3fa819825c.

2   "Brian Wansink," Faculty Profile, Cornell University, accessed on
July 13, 2017, https://dyson.cornell.edu/people/brian-wansink.

3   Brian Wansink, *Mindless Eating: Why We Eat More Than We
Think* (New York: Bantam Books, 2007), 16–18.

4   Ibid, 1.

5   "How Technology is Changing the Way We Sleep," National
Sleep Foundation, accessed on August 15, 2017, https://sleep
.org/articles/how-technology-changing-the-way-we-sleep/.

6   "PNAS study: using iPad before bed has major impact on
sleep," f.lux, accessed on August 22, 2017, https://justgetflux
.com/news/2014/12/22/study.html; Anne-Marie Chang et al.,
"Evening use of light-emitting eReaders negatively affects sleep,
circadian timing, and next-morning alertness," *Proceedings of
the National Academy of Sciences* 112, no. 4 (January 2015):
1232–7, http://www.pnas.org/content/112/4/1232.full.pdf.

7   Ibid.

8 "See," National Sleep Foundation, accessed on August 15, 2017, https://sleepfoundation.org/bedroom/see.php.

9 "The Ideal Temperature for Sleep," National Sleep Foundation, accessed on August 15, 2017, https://sleep.org/articles/temperature-for-sleep/.

10 "Touch," National Sleep Foundation, National Sleep Foundation, accessed on August 15, 2017, https://sleepfoundation.org/bedroom/touch.php.

11 Brian Wansink, *Slim By Design: Mindless Eating Solutions for Everyday Life*, (New York: William Morrow, 2014), 36–37.

12 Ibid, 37.

13 "Precision Nutrition Approved: Our favorite nutritional supplements," Precision Nutrition, accessed on August 23, 2017, http://www.precisionnutrition.com/supplements.

14 "Sitting and Chair Design," Cornell University Ergonomics Web, accessed on August 25, 2017, http://ergo.human.cornell.edu/dea3250flipbook/dea3250notes/sitting.html.

15 "The truth about email: What's a normal inbox?" Pando, accessed on August 13, 2017, https://pando.com/2013/04/05/the-truth-about-email-whats-a-normal-inbox/.

16 Darren Hardy, *The Compound Effect: Jumpstart Your Income, Your Life, and Your Success* (Dallas: Success Media, 2010), 130–131.

17 "Who We Are," Achilles International, accessed on August 2, 2017, https://www.achillesinternational.org/who-we-are/.

18 Chip Heath and Dan Heath. *Switch: How to Change Things When Change Is Hard*, (New York: Broadway Books, 2010), 227.

19 Ibid.; Nicholas A. Christakis, "The Spread of Obesity in a Large Social Network over 32 Years," New England Journal of Medicine 357 (2007): 370–379.

20 Susan Krauss Whitbourne, "5 Reasons Why Clutter Is Bad for Your Mental Health," *Psychology Today*, May 13, 2017, https://www.psychologytoday.com/blog/fulfillment-any-age/201705/5-reasons-why-clutter-is-bad-your-mental-health.

21 Meg Sullivan, "Trouble in paradise: UCLA book enumer-
    ates challenges faced by middle-class L.A. families." UCLA
    Newsroom, June 19, 2012, http://newsroom.ucla.edu/releases/
    trouble-in-paradise-new-ucla-book.
22 Michael Blanding, "Psychology: Your Attention, Please," Princ-
    eton Alumni Weekly, accessed on August 6, 2017, https://paw
    .princeton.edu/article/psychology-your-attention-please.

CHAPTER 5

1   Jocko Willink and Leif Babin, *Extreme Ownership: How
    U.S. Navy Seals Lead and Win* (New York: St. Martin's Press,
    2015), 274.
2   "Frequently Monitoring Progress Toward Goals Increases
    Chance of Success," American Psychological Association, Octo-
    ber 28, 2015, http://www.apa.org/news/press/releases/2015/10/
    progress-goals.aspx.
3   Minjung Koo and Ayelet Fishbach, "The Small-Area Hypoth-
    esis: Effects of Progress Monitoring on Goal Adherence," *Jour-
    nal of Consumer Research*, Vol. 39, No. 3 (October 2012), pp.
    493–509.
4   Hardy, *The Compound Effect*, 37.
5   Mihaly Csikszentmihalyi, *Flow: The Psychology of Optimal
    Experience* (New York: Harper Perennial, 1990), 3.
6   Sam Shank, "How to Trick Yourself Into Becoming a Morning
    Person," LinkedIn page, May 5, 2016, https://www.linkedin.com/
    pulse/how-trick-yourself-becoming-morning-person-sam-shank.

CHAPTER 6

1. Daniel J. DeNoon, "Diets Don't Work Long-Term," WebMD,
    April 11, 2007, http://www.webmd.com/diet/news/20070411/
    diets-dont-work-long-term#1.
2. John Berardi, "11 things I've learned coaching elite and
    professional athletes," Precision Nutrition, accessed on
    August 7, 2017, http://www.precisionnutrition.com/coaching-
    elite-and-professional-athletes.

3. John Berardi, "Paleo, vegan, intermittent fasting... Here's how to choose the absolute best diet for you," Precision Nutrition, accessed on June 23, 2017, http://www.precisionnutrition.com/the-best-diet.

4. https://www.discovery.com/tv-shows/dual-survival/

5. John Berardi, "Experiments with Intermittent Fasting," Precision Nutrition, accessed on August 27, 2017, https://www.precisionnutrition.com/intermittent-fasting.

6. John Berardi, "Intermittent Fasting: Who's It For? (And, if It's Not for You, What to Do Instead)," *HuffPost*, December 3, 2014, https://www.huffingtonpost.com/john-berardi-phd/intermittent-fasting-whos_b_6236712.html.

7. Ibid.

8. By the Editors of *Eat This, Not That!*, "The Best and Worst Milks and Milk Alternatives," Eat This, Not That!, accessed on June 27, 2017, http://www.eatthis.com/best-worst-milk-alternatives.

9. "What is Lactose Intolerance?," Physicians Committee for Responsible Medicine, accessed on June 27, 2017, http://www.pcrm.org/health/diets/vegdiets/what-is-lactose-intolerance.

10. By the Editors of *Eat This, Not That!*, "The Best and Worst Milks and Milk Alternatives," Eat This, Not That!, accessed on June 27, 2017, http://www.eatthis.com/best-worst-milk-alternatives.

11. Michael J. Breus, "New Details on Caffeine's Sleep-Disrupting Effects," *Psychology Today*, December 16, 2013, https://www.psychologytoday.com/blog/sleep-newzzz/201312/new-details-caffeine-s-sleep-disrupting-effects; Christopher Drake et al., "Caffeine effects on sleep taken 0, 3, or 6 hours before going to bed," *Journal of Clinical Sleep Medicine* 9, no. 11 (November 2013): 1195–1200.

12. Brian Wansink, *Mindless Eating: Why We Eat More Than We Think* (New York: Bantam Books, 2007), 1.

13. "Introducing Binge John," T-Mobile, accessed on August 23, 2017, http://t-mobilebingejohn.com/.

14. Megan Orciari, "Beverage companies still target kids with marketing for unhealthy, sugary drinks," Yale News, November 19, 2014, https://news.yale.edu/2014/11/19/beverage-companies-still-target-kids-marketing-unhealthy-sugary-drinks.

15. "Nutritional Information," IHOP, accessed on June 27, 2017, https://www.ihop.com/nutritional-info.

16. "Lay's Potato Chips," Frito Lay, accessed on June 27, 2017, http://www.fritolay.com/snacks/product-page/lays.

17. "Lowfat Yogurt," Dannon, accessed on June 27, 2017, http://www.dannonyogurt.com/yogurt/lowfat-yogurt/vanilla; "Nutritional Information," Yoplait, accessed on June 27, 2017, http://www.yoplait.com/product/mix-ins-very-berry-crisp.

18. "Reese's Pieces Candy," Reese's, accessed on June 27, 2017, https://www.hersheys.com/reeses/en_us/products/reeses-pieces-candy.html.

19. "Whey Protein Bar," Gatorade, accessed on June 27, 2017, https://shop.gatorade.com/sports-fuel/whey-protein-bar; "Nutritional Information," Snickers, accessed on June 27, 2017, https://www.snickers.com/nutritional-info.

20. "Salt," Centers for Disease Control and Prevention, accessed on June 27, 2017, https://www.cdc.gov/salt/index.htm.

21. BJ Gaddour, Men's Health Your Body is Your Barbell (New York: Rodale, 2014), 13.

22. Brian St. Pierre, "The best calorie control guide. [Infographic]," Precision Nutrition, accessed on August 1, 2017, http://www.precisionnutrition.com/calorie-control-guide-infographic; John Berardi, "Create the perfect meal with this simple 5-step guide. [Infographic]," Precision Nutrition, accessed on August 1, 2017, http://www.precisionnutrition.com/create-the-perfect-meal-infographic.

23. Brian St. Pierre, "The best calorie control guide. [Infographic]," Precision Nutrition, accessed on August 1, 2017, http://www.precisionnutrition.com/calorie-control-guide-infographic; John Berardi, "Create the perfect meal with this simple 5-step guide. [Infographic]," Precision Nutrition,

accessed on August 1, 2017, http://www.precisionnutrition .com/create-the-perfect-meal-infographic.

24. Brian St. Pierre, "Carb Controversy," Precision Nutrition, accessed on August 1, 2017, http://www.precisionnutrition.com/ low-carb-diets.

25. Brian St. Pierre, "The best calorie control guide. [Info-graphic]," Precision Nutrition, accessed on August 1, 2017, http://www.precisionnutrition.com/calorie-control-guide-infographic; John Berardi, "Create the perfect meal with this simple 5-step guide. [Infographic]," Precision Nutrition, accessed on August 1, 2017, http://www.precisionnutrition.com/ create-the-perfect-meal-infographic.

26. Ryan Andrews, "All About Healthy Fats," Precision Nutrition, accessed on August 1, 2017, http://www.precisionnutrition .com/all-about-healthy-fats.

27. Brian St. Pierre, "The best calorie control guide. [Infographic]," Precision Nutrition, accessed on August 1, 2017, http://www .precisionnutrition.com/calorie-control-guide-infographic; John Berardi, "Create the perfect meal with this simple 5-step guide. [Infographic]," Precision Nutrition, accessed on August 1, 2017, http://www.precisionnutrition.com/ create-the-perfect-meal-infographic.

28. John Berardi, "Create the perfect meal with this simple 5-step guide. [Infographic]," Precision Nutrition, accessed on August 1, 2017, http://www.precisionnutrition.com/create-the-perfect-meal-infographic.

29. Brian St. Pierre, "The best calorie control guide. [Info-graphic]," Precision Nutrition, accessed on August 1, 2017, http://www.precisionnutrition.com/calorie-control-guide-infographic; John Berardi, "Create the perfect meal with this simple 5-step guide. [Infographic]," Precision Nutrition, accessed on August 1, 2017, http://www.precisionnutrition .com/create-the-perfect-meal-infographic.

30. Brian St. Pierre, "Workout nutrition explained," Precision Nutrition, accessed on August 1, 2017, http://www.precision-nutrition.com/workout-nutrition-explained.

CHAPTER 7

[1]   John J. Ratey, with Eric Hagerman, *Spark: The Revolution-
     ary New Science of Exercise and the Brain* (New York: Little,
     Brown & Company, 2008), 245.

[2]   Ron Friedman, "Regular Exercise Is Part of Your Job," *Harvard
     Business Review*, October 3, 2014, https://hbr.org/2014/10/
     regular-exercise-is-part-of-your-job; Hogan et al., "Exercise
     holds immediate benefits for affect and cognition in younger
     and older adults," *Psychology and Aging* 28, no. 2 (June 2013):
     587–594.

[3]   Molly McElroy, "Exercise shown to reverse brain deterioration
     brought on by aging," *Illinois News Bureau*, November 20,
     2006, https://news.illinois.edu/blog/view/6367/206797.

[4]   "ACSM Issues New Recommendations on Quantity and Quality
     of Exercise," ACSM, accessed on August 4, 2017, http://www
     .acsm.org/about-acsm/media-room/news-releases/2011/08/01/
     acsm-issues-new-recommendations-on-quantity-and-quality-
     of-exercise.

[5]   "ACSM Issues New Recommendations on Quantity and Quality
     of Exercise," ACSM, accessed on August 4, 2017, http://www
     .acsm.org/about-acsm/media-room/news-releases/2011/08/01/
     acsm-issues-new-recommendations-on-quantity-and-quality-
     of-exercise.

[6]   Carl Foster and John Pocari with Mark Anders, "ACE-Spon-
     sored Research: Exploring the Effects of Music on Exercise
     Intensity," ACE, accessed on June 11, 2017, https://www.acefit-
     ness.org/certifiednews/images/article/pdfs/MusicStudy.pdf.

[7]   "Dr. Karageorghis reveals science behind Spotify Ultimate
     Workout Playlist," Brunel University London, January 16, 2014,
     https://www.brunel.ac.uk/news-and-events/news/articles/Dr-
     Karageorghis-reveals-science-behind-Spotify-Ultimate-Work-
     out-Playlist.

[8]   Amanda MacMillan, "How Your Smartphone Ruins Your
     Workout," Time Health, January 18, 2017, http://time
     .com/4637895/exercise-smartphone-workout/; Michael J. Rebold
     et al., "The impact of cell phone texting on the amount of time

spent exercising at different intensities," *Computers in Human Behavior* 55, Part A (February 2016): 167-171.

9 "ACSM Information On ... High-Intensity Interval Training," ACSM, accessed on July 17, 2017, https://www.acsm.org/docs/brochures/high-intensity-interval-training.pdf.

10 "Measuring Physical Activity Intensity, Centers for Disease Control and Prevention, accessed on July 17, 2017, https://www.cdc.gov/physicalactivity/basics/measuring/index.html.

11 Schuler, Lou and Alwyn Cosgrove. *The New Rules of Lifting Supercharged: Ten All-New Programs for Men and Women* (New York: Avery, 2013), 15.

12 "National Center for Health Statistics," Centers for Disease Control and Prevention, accessed on August 6, 2017, https://www.cdc.gov/nchs/fastats/exercise.htm.

13 Tae Nyun Kim et al., "Sarcopenia: Definition, Epidemiology, and Pathophysiology," *Journal of Bone Metabolism*, (May 2013): 1–10, https://doi.org/10.11005/jbm.2013.20.1.1.

14 Amanda Woerner, "Strength Training May Help Keep You Young, Study Shows," Daily Burn, October 27, 2014, http://dailyburn.com/life/fitness/strength-training-aging-study-100714/.

15 John J. Ratey, with Eric Hagerman, *Spark: The Revolutionary New Science of Exercise and the* Brain (New York: Little, Brown & Company, 2008), 257.

16 Jenna B. Gillen et al., "Twelve Weeks of Sprint Interval Training Improves Indices of Cardiometabolic Health Similar to Traditional Endurance Training despite a Five-Fold Lower Exercise Volume and Time Commitment," *PLOS ONE*, (April 2016), https://doi.org/10.1371/journal.pone.0154075.

17 "Frequently Asked Questions," Orangetheory Fitness, accessed on August 29, 2017, https://www.orangetheoryfitness.com/faq.

CHAPTER 8

1 Leslie Perlow and Jessica L. Porter, "Making Time Off Predictable—and Required." *Harvard Business Review* 87, no. 10 (October 2009), https://hbr.org/2009/10/making-time-off-predictable-and-required.

2 Ibid.

3   Steve Lohr, "Slow Down, Brave Multitasker, and Don't Read This in Traffic," *New York Times*, March 25, 2007, http://www.nytimes.com/2007/03/25/business/25multi.html?mcubz=3.

4   Jacqui Bealing, "Brain scans reveal 'grey matter' differences in media multitaskers," University of Sussex, September 25, 2014, http://www.sussex.ac.uk/broadcast/read/26540.

5   Amanda, Schupak, "Stressed? Close your email," CBS News, December 9, 2014, https://www.cbsnews.com/news/stressed-close-your-email/; Kostadin Kushlev, "Checking email less frequently reduces stress," *Computers in Human Behavior* Volume 43 (February 2015): 220–228.

6   "the human era @ work; Findings from The Energy Project and Harvard Business Review," The Energy Project, accessed on August 11, 2017.

7   Kristin Morales, "Skip the caffeine, opt for the stairs to feel more energized," University of Georgia, April 19, 2017, http://news.uga.edu/releases/article/stairs-more-energy-research/.

8   "the human era @ work; Findings from The Energy Project and Harvard Business Review," The Energy Project, accessed on August 11, 2017.

9   Julia Gifford, "The Rule of 52 and 17: It's Random, But it Ups Your Productivity," The Muse, accessed on August 12, 2017, https://www.themuse.com/advice/the-rule-of-52-and-17-its-random-but-it-ups-your-productivity.

10   SUCCESS Staff, "7 Work Habits of The Rich and Genius," *SUCCESS*, accessed on August 24, 2017, http://www.success.com/article/7-work-habits-the-rich-and-genius.

11   "Just One-in-Five Employees Take Actual Lunch Break," Right Management, accessed on August 28, 2017, http://www.right.com/wps/wcm/connect/right-us-en/home/thoughtwire/categories/media-center/Just+OneinFive+Employees+Take+Actual+Lunch+Break.

12   "On-Time Performance - Flight Delays at a Glance," Bureau of Transportation Statistics, accessed on August 25, 2017, https://www.transtats.bts.gov/HomeDrillChart.asp.

13 Marguerite Ward, "28-year-old CEO who's taken 500 flights shares his No. 1 travel tip," CNBC, April 6, 2017, https://www.cnbc.com/2017/04/06/28-year-old-ceo-whos-taken-500-flights-shares-his-no-1-travel-tip.html?view=story&%24DEVICE%24=native-android-mobile.

14 "Sitting and Chair Design," Cornell University Ergonomics Web, accessed on August 25, 2017, http://ergo.human.cornell.edu/dea3250flipbook/dea3250notes/sitting.html.

CHAPTER 9

1 A.M. Williamson and Anne-Marie Feyer, "Moderate sleep deprivation produces impairments in cognitive and motor performance equivalent to legally prescribed levels of alcohol intoxication," *Occupational and Environmental Medicine* 57 (2000), 649–655, https://www.ncbi.nlm.nih.gov/pmc/articles/PMC1739867/pdf/v057p00649.pdf.

2 Marshall Goldsmith with Mark Reiter, *What Got You Here Won't Get You There: How Successful People Become Even More Successful* (New York: Hyperion, 2007), 16.

3 Arianna Huffington, *Thrive: The Third Metric to Redefining Success and Creating a Life of Well-Being, Wisdom, and Wonder* (New York: Harmony Books, 2014), 74.

4 Shawn Stevenson. *Sleep Smarter: 21 Essential Strategies to Sleep Your Way to a Better Body, Better Health, and Bigger Success* (New York: Rodale, 2016), 42; Kulreet Chaudhary, "Sleep and Longevity," The Dr. Oz Show, May 27, 2011, http://www.doctoroz.com/blog/kulreet-chaudhary-md/sleep-and-longevity.

5 "Reading 'can help reduce stress,'" *The Telegraph*, March 30, 2009, http://www.telegraph.co.uk/news/health/news/5070874/Reading-can-help-reduce-stress.html.

6 "PNAS study: using iPad before bed has major impact on sleep," f.lux, accessed on August 22, 2017, https://justgetflux.com/news/2014/12/22/study.html; Anne-Marie Chang et al., "Evening use of light-emitting eReaders negatively affects sleep, circadian timing, and next-morning alertness," *Proceedings of*

the National Academy of Sciences 112, no. 4 (January 2015): 1232–1237, http://www.pnas.org/content/112/4/1232.full.pdf.

7   Linda Wasmer Andrews, "How Gratitude Helps You Sleep at Night," Psychology Today, November 9, 2011, https://www.psychologytoday.com/blog/minding-the-body/201111/how-gratitude-helps-you-sleep-night; Nancy Digdon et al., "Effects of Constructive Worry, Imagery Distraction, and Gratitude Interventions on Sleep Quality: A Pilot Trial," *Applied Psychology*: Health *and Well-Being* 3, no. 2 (July 2011): 193–206.

8   "Healthy Sleep Tips," National Sleep Foundation, accessed on August 14, 2017, https://sleepfoundation.org/sleep-tools-tips/healthy-sleep-tips/page/0/1.

9   Lynn Celmer, "Study suggests that what you eat can influence how you sleep," American Academy of Sleep Medicine, January 14, 2016, http://www.aasmnet.org/articles.aspx?id=6072.

10   "National Sleep Foundation Recommends New Sleep Times," National Sleep Foundation, February 2, 2015, https://sleepfoundation.org/press-release/national-sleep-foundation-recommends-new-sleep-times.

11   "Couples Sleeping Separately: Bad For the Relationship?," National Sleep Foundation, accessed on August 28, 2017, https://sleepfoundation.org/sites/default/files/subscription/sub003.txt.sleep-times.

12   Laura Vanderkam, *What the Most Successful People Do Before Breakfast* (New York: Portfolio/Penguin, 2013), 7.

13   Tony Robbins, "Tony Robbins: 'Gratitude Is the Solution to Anger and Fear," Thrive Global, November 30, 2016, https://journal.thriveglobal.com/tony-robbins-gratitude-is-the-solution-to-anger-and-fear-c3fa819825c.

14   Ibid.

15   Sam Shank, "How to Trick Yourself Into Becoming a Morning Person," LinkedIn page, May 5, 2016, https://www.linkedin.com/pulse/how-trick-yourself-becoming-morning-person-sam-shank.

16   "From Home to Work, the Average Commute is 26.4 Minutes," Bureau of Transportation Statistics, October 2003, https://

www.rita.dot.gov/bts/sites/rita.dot.gov.bts/files/publications/ omnistats/volume_03_issue_04/pdf/entire.pdf.

17   Evan Halper and Michael Rothfeld, "This Puts Your Commute to Shame," *Los Angeles Times*, March 7, 2008, http://articles .latimes.com/2008/mar/07/local/me-arnold7.

18   David Wilkes, "Britain's worst commute: Father has SIX-HOUR round trip to work every day… clocking up 100,000 miles a year," *Daily Mail*, January 29, 2014, http://www.dailymail .co.uk/news/article-2547962/Britains-worst-commute-Father-SIX- HOUR-round-trip-work-day-clocking-100-000-miles-year.html.

19   Neha Gothe et al., "The Acute Effects of Yoga on Executive Function," *Journal of Physical Activity & Health*, (May 2013): 488- 495, http://www.academia.edu/3145421/The_Acute_Effects_ of_Yoga_on_Executive_Function.

20   Timothy McCall, "38 Health Benefits of Yoga," Yoga Journal, August 28, 2007, https://www.yogajournal.com/lifestyle/ count-yoga-38-ways-yoga-keeps-fit.

21   "What is Meditation and Mindfulness?", Headspace, accessed on August 11, 2017, https://help.headspace.com/hc/en-us/articles /218913037-What-is-meditation-and-mindfulness.

CHAPTER 10

1   "Health Care Costs Steadily Increase with Body Mass," Duke Global Health Institute, December 16, 2013, http:// globalhealth.duke.edu/media/news/health-care-costs- steadily-increase-body-mass.

2   "National Center for Health Statistics," Centers for Disease Control and Prevention, accessed on June 28, 2017, https:// www.cdc.gov/nchs/fastats/obesity-overweight.htm.

3   Dan Witters and Sangeeta Agrawal, "Unhealthy U.S. Workers' Absenteeism Costs $153 Billion," Gallup, October 17, 2011, http://www.gallup.com/poll/150026/unhealthy-workers-absen- teeism-costs-153-billion.aspx.

4   "The cost of presenteeism – and how to fix it," Virgin Pulse, March 8, 2016, https://globalchallenge.virginpulse.com/blog/ the-cost-of-presenteeism.

5   Robert Ferris, "More than 2 billion people are overweight or obese worldwide, says study," CNBC, June 12, 2017, https://www.cnbc.com/2017/06/12/more-than-2-billion-people-are-overweight-or-obese-worldwide-says-study.html.

6   Leigh Stringer, *The Healthy Workplace: How to Improve the Well-Being of Your Employees- and Boost Your Company's Bottom Line* (New York: AMACOM, 2016) 12; Katherine Baicker et al., "Workplace wellness programs can generate savings," *Health Affairs* 29, no.2 (2010): 304-311, https://dash.harvard.edu/handle/1/5345879.

7   Larry Senn and Jim Delaney. *Winning Teams Winning Cultures* (Long Beach: Leadership Press, 2006), 37.

8   Harold D. Stolovitch and Erica J. Keeps, *Telling Ain't Training* (Alexandria: ASTD Press, 2011), 53.

9   Ibid.

10   Alfie Kohn, *Punished by Rewards: The Trouble with Gold Stars, Incentive Plans, A's, Praise and Other Bribes* (New York: Houghton Mifflin Company, 1993), 76.

11   Daniel, H. Pink, *Drive: The Surprising Truth About What Motivates Us* (New York: Riverhead Books, 2012), 37; Edward L. Deci et al., "A Meta-Analytic Review of Experiments Examining the Effects of Extrinsic Rewards on Intrinsic Motivation," *Psychological Bulletin* 125, no. 6 (1999): 659.

12   "Companies Trimming Fat While Fattening Wallets," Fox Business Network, February 22, 2013, http://video.foxbusiness.com/v/2182852983001/#sp=show-clips.

13   Ibid.

14   Tom Gardner, "6 Ways to Save Your Life -- and Your Company," LinkedIn page, May 29, 2014, https://www.linkedin.com/pulse/20140529152729-42170371-6-ways-to-save-your-life-and-your-company.

15   Alfie Kohn, *Punished by Rewards*, 76.

16   Laszlo Bock, *Work Rules!: Insights from Inside Google That Will Transform How You Live and Lead* (New York: Twelve, 2015), 313.

17   Ibid.

[18] Kristin Morales, "Skip the caffeine, opt for the stairs to feel more energized," University of Georgia, April 19, 2017, http://news.uga.edu/releases/article/stairs-more-energy-research/.

[19] Joseph Barberio, "10 Companies With Incredible Office Health and Wellness Zones," Working Mother, March 2, 2017, http://www.workingmother.com/10-companies-with-health-and-wellness-zones.

[20] Ryan Holmes, "5 (budget) hacks for building amazing office culture," LinkedIn page, November 22, 2016, https://www.linkedin.com/pulse/5-budget-hacks-building-amazing-office-culture-ryan-holmes.

[21] "121 Employee Wellness Program Ideas For Your Office (+10 Bonus Ideas)," Snack Nation, accessed on August 15, 2017, http://www.snacknation.com/wp-content/uploads/2015/12/121-Corporate-Wellness-Program-Ideas-For-Your-Office-Bonus.pdf?mkt_tok=eyJpIjoiWWiVMo1tTXpaamswWlRBeCIsInQiOiJTZkphRWFYaUhnbWRqWlNVS2Y3MENSbUhTSWtSTlV4QW9OdUVSRUludnVpYiNLYiNpa2NUOVN-QZHJlcU9OdkJzeXZPZlk2XC9ndHltlc293dDDdSdllRNDB-HamR2M1BJeVRoeXhlT2ZFYWo2aoRGUVU5bXJRX-C9oRzZYNmR0VmJtaWFWWlno%3D.

[22] Nina McQueen, "Wellness, unleashing greatness at LinkedIn–Part 7," LinkedIn page, July 16, 2016, https://www.linkedin.com/pulse/wellness-unleashing-greatness-linkedinpart-7-nina-mcqueen?published=u.

[23] Ibid.

[24] Ibid.

[25] Nina McQueen, "InDay: Investing In Our Employees So They Can Invest In Themselves," LinkedIn, July 29, 2015, https://blog.linkedin.com/2015/07/29/inday-investing-in-our-employees-so-they-can-invest-in-themselves.

[26] Jennifer Fisher, "Who doesn't want well-being?," LinkedIn page, May 31, 2017, https://www.linkedin.com/pulse/who-doesnt-want-well-being-jennifer-fisher.

27   Jason Fried, "Unusual employee benefits at Basecamp - the complete list," LinkedIn page, January 23, 2017, https://www.linkedin.com/pulse/employee-benefits-basecamp-complete-list-jason-fried.

28   *"Working Well: A Global Survey of Workforce Well-being Strategies*," Xerox, accessed on August 22, 2017, http://www.globalhealthyworkplace.org/casestudies/2016_Global_Well-being_Survey_Executive-Summary.pdf.

LIST OF AUTHOR INTERVIEWS

Pete Leibman conducted the following interviews for this book.

Author interview (via phone) with Kevin Hart: December 5, 2016.

Author interview (via phone) with Chris Tsakalakis: December 7, 2016.

Author interview (via phone) with Rhonda Vetere: January 4, 2017.

Author interview (via phone) with Josh Riff: January 16, 2017.

Author interview (via phone) with Dick Costolo: January 17, 2017.

Author interview (via phone) with Hoby Darling: January 26, 2017.

Author interview (via phone) with Ken Lubin: April 4, 2017.

Author interview (via phone) with Michelle Kluz: April 12, 2017.

Author interview (via phone) with Don Monistere: April 14, 2017.

Author interview (via email) with Wyatt Everhart: April 26, 2017.

Author interview (via phone) with Mukesh Aghi: May 2, 2017.

Author interview (via phone) with Elliott Ferguson: May 4, 2017.

Author interview (via phone) with Juan Uro: May 5, 2017.

Author interview (via phone) with Tom Lokar: May 16, 2017.

Author interview (via phone) with Sam Abbitt: May 16, 2017.

Author interview (via email) with Jeff Stibel: May 17, 2017.

Author interview (via phone) with Rhonda Germany-Ballintyn: May 24, 2017.

Author interview (via phone) with Kent Wuthrich: May 26, 2017.

Author interview (via phone) with Joseph Callahan: May 31, 2017.

Author interview (via phone) with Sarah Kalamchi: June 2, 2017.

Author interview (via phone) with Jennifer Carr-Smith: June 9, 2017.

Author interview (via phone) with Larry Senn: June 9, 2017.

Author interview (via email) with Steven Sinofsky: June 9, 2017.

Author interview (via email) with Kristin Machacek Leary: June 10, 2017.

Author interview (via phone) with Daniel Johnston: June 12, 2017.

Author interview (via phone) with Barbara Tulipane: June 22, 2017.

Author interview (via phone) with Strauss Zelnick: June 23, 2017.

Author interview (via phone) with Alex Douzet: June 23, 2017.

Author interview (via phone) with Tara-Nicholle Nelson, June 29, 2017.

Author interview (via phone) with Jennifer Fisher: June 30, 2017.

Author interview (via phone) with Frank Karbe: June 30, 2017.

Author interview (via phone) with David Inns: July 5, 2017.

Author interview (via phone) with Bob Fleshner: July 5, 2017.

Author interview (via phone) with Sam Shank: July 12, 2017.

Author interview (via phone) with Janine Allis: July 12, 2017.

Author interview (via phone) with Chip Bergh: July 14, 2017.

Author interview (via phone) with Robin Thurston: July 14, 2017.

Author interview (via phone) with Amy Cozad Magaña: July 20, 2017.

Author interview (via phone) with Emily Kolakowski: July 21, 2017.

Author interview (via phone) with Laurie Coe: July 21, 2017.

Author interview (via phone) with Penny Pritzker: August 2, 2017.

Author interview (via phone) with Scott O'Neil: August 3, 2017.

Author interview (via phone) with Bahram Akradi: August 9, 2017.

Author interview (via phone) with Dave Long: August 18, 2017.

Author interview (via phone) with Jonathan Edelheit: August 21, 2017.

BIBLIOGRAPHY

ACE Personal Trainer Manual: The Ultimate Resource for Fitness Professionals (Third Edition). San Diego: American Council on Exercise, 2003.

Ariely, Dan. *Predictably Irrational: The Hidden Forces That Shape Our Decisions.* New York: Harper Perennial, 2008.

Baumeister, Roy F. & John Tierney. *Willpower: Rediscovering the Greatest Human Strength.* New York: Penguin Books, 2011.

Berardi, John and Ryan Andrews. *The Essentials of Sport and Exercise Nutrition: Certification Manual* (Second Edition). Precision Nutrition, Inc., 2016.

Bilas, Jay. *Toughness: Developing True Strength On and Off the Court.* New York: New American Library, 2014.

Bock, Laszlo. *Work Rules!: Insights from Inside Google That Will Transform How You Live and Lead.* New York: Twelve, 2015.

Buettner, Dan. *The Blue Zones Solution: Eating and Living Like the World's Healthiest People.* Washington, D.C.: National Geographic, 2015.

Burchard. Brendon. *High Performance Habits: How Extraordinary People Become That Way.* Carlsbad: Hay House, Inc., 2017.

Burchard, Brendon. *The Charge: Activating the 10 Human Drives That Make You Feel Alive.* New York: Free Press, 2012.

Canfield, Jack. *The Success Principles: How to Get from Where You Are to Where You Want to Be.* New York: Collins, 2005.

Covey, Stephen R. *The 7 Habits of Highly Effective People: Restoring the Character Ethic.* New York: Simon & Schuster, 1989.

Csikszentmihalyi, Mihaly. *Flow: The Psychology of Optimal Experience.* New York: Harper Perennial, 1990.

Dean, Jeremy. *Making Habits, Breaking Habits: Why We Do Things, Why We Don't, and How to Make any Change Stick.* Boston: Da Capo Press, 2013.

Deci, Edward L. with Richard Flaste. *Why We Do What We Do: Understanding Self-Motivation.* New York: Penguin Books, 1995.

Duckworth, Angela. *Grit: The Power of Passion and Perseverance.* New York: Scribner, 2016.

Dweck, Carol S. *Mindset: The New Psychology of Success.* New York: Ballantine Books, 2006.

Duhigg, Charles. *The Power of Habit: Why We Do What We Do in Life and Business.* New York: Random House Trade Paperbacks, 2014.

Fried, Jason and David Heinemeier Hansson. *Rework.* New York: Crown Business, 2010.

Gaddour, BJ. *Men's Health Your Body is Your Barbell.* New York: Rodale, 2014.

Gelles, David. *Mindful Work: How Meditation Is Changing Business from the Inside Out.* Boston: First Mariner Books, 2016.

Goldsmith, Marshall with Mark Reiter. *What Got You Here Won't Get You There: How Successful People Become Even More Successful.* New York: Hyperion, 2007.

Griessman, B. Eugene. *Time Tactics of Very Successful People.* New York: McGraw-Hill, Inc, 1994.

Groppel, Jack L. with Bob Andelman. *The Corporate Athlete: How to Achieve Maximal Performance in Business and Life.* New York: John Wiley & Sons, Inc., 2000.

Hardy, Darren. *The Compound Effect: Jumpstart Your Income, Your Life, and Your Success.* Dallas: Success Media, 2010.

Heath, Chip and Dan Heath. *Decisive: How to Make Better Choices In Life and Work.* New York: Crown Business, 2013.

Heath, Chip and Dan Heath. *Switch: How to Change Things When Change Is Hard.* New York: Broadway Books, 2010.

Huffington, Arianna. *The Sleep Revolution: Transforming Your Life, One Night at a Time.* New York: Harmony Books, 2016.

Huffington, Arianna. *Thrive: The Third Metric to Redefining Success and Creating a Life of Well-Being, Wisdom, and Wonder.* New York: Harmony Books, 2014.

Kohn, Alfie. *Punished by Rewards: The Trouble with Gold Stars, Incentive Plans, A's, Praise and Other Bribes.* New York: Houghton Mifflin Company, 1993.

Leibman, Pete. *I Got My Dream Job and So Can You: 7 Steps to Creating Your Ideal Career After College.* New York: AMACOM, 2012.

Loehr, Jim and Tony Schwartz. *The Power of Full Engagement: Managing Energy, Not Time, Is the Key to High Performance and Personal Renewal.* New York: Free Press Paperbacks, 2003.

McGonigal, Kelly. *The Willpower Instinct: How Self-Control Works, Why It Matters, and What You Can Do to Get More of It.* New York: Avery, 2012.

Mischel, Walter. *The Marshmallow Test: Understanding Self-Control and How to Master It.* London: Bantam Press, 2014.

Newport, Cal. *Deep Work; Rules for Focused Success in a Distracted World.* New York: Grand Central Publishing, 2016.

Pink, Daniel, H. *Drive: The Surprising Truth About What Motivates Us.* New York: Riverhead Books, 2012.

Ratey, John J. with Eric Hagerman, *Spark: The Revolutionary New Science of Exercise and the Brain.* New York: Little, Brown & Company, 2008.

Reinhard, Tonia. *Superfoods: The Healthiest Foods on the Planet.* Buffalo, Firefly Books, 2010.

Rubin, Gretchen. *Better Than Before: Mastering the Habits of Our Everyday Lives.* New York: Crown Publishers, 2015.

Schuler, Lou and Alwyn Cosgrove. *The New Rules of Lifting Supercharged: Ten All-New Programs for Men and Women.* New York: Avery, 2013.

Schwartz, Tony with Jean Gomes and Catherine McCarthy. *Be Excellent at Anything: The Four Keys to Transforming the Way We Work and Live.* New York: Free Press, 2010.

Seligman, Martin E.P. *Learned Optimism: How to Change Your Mind and Your Life.* New York: Vintage Books, 2006.

Senn, Larry and Jim Delaney. *Winning Teams Winning Cultures.* Long Beach: Leadership Press, 2006.

Stephano, Renee-Marie and Jonathan Edelheit. *Engaging Wellness: Corporate Wellness Programs That Work.* Corporate Health and Wellness Association, 2012.

Stevenson, Shawn. *Sleep Smarter: 21 Essential Strategies to Sleep Your Way to a Better Body, Better Health, and Bigger Success.* New York: Rodale, 2016.

Stolovitch, Harold D. and Erica J. Keeps, *Telling Ain't Training.* Alexandria: ASTD Press, 2011.

Stringer, Leigh. *The Healthy Workplace: How to Improve the Well-Being of Your Employees—and Boost Your Company's Bottom Line.* New York: AMACOM, 2016.

Thaler, Richard H. and Cass R. Sunstein. *Nudge: Improving Decisions About Health, Wealth, and Happiness.* New York: Penguin, 2009.

Tracy, Brian. *Maximum Achievement: Strategies and Skills That Will Unlock Your Hidden Powers to Succeed.* New York: Simon & Schuster, 1993.

Vanderkam, Laura. *What the Most Successful People Do Before Breakfast.* New York: Portfolio/Penguin, 2013.

Wansink, Brian. *Mindless Eating: Why We Eat More Than We Think.* New York: Bantam Books, 2007.

Wansink, Brian. *Slim By Design: Mindless Eating Solutions for Everyday Life.* New York: William Morrow, 2014.

Willink, Jocko and Leif Babin. *Extreme Ownership: How U.S. Navy Seals Lead and Win.* New York: St. Martin's Press, 2015.

Wiseman, Richard. *The Luck Factor: Changing Your Luck, Changing Your Life: The Four Essential Principles.* New York: Miramax Books, 2003.

Workman, Jennifer. *Stop Your Cravings: Satisfy Your Tastes Without Sacrificing Your Health.* New York: The Free Press, 2002.

ACKNOWLEDGMENTS

This book was only possible due to the support of many other people. First and foremost, this book is dedicated to my Mom, my Dad, and my brother Matt. Thank you for always supporting me and all of my dreams. Words could never express how much I love you and appreciate you.

Thank you to my agent Grace Freedson and to everyone at Skyhorse Publishing for making this book possible.

Thank you to all of the people who made time for me to interview them for this book (including Sam Abbitt, Mukesh Aghi, Bahram Akradi, Janine Allis, Chip Bergh, Joseph Callahan, Jennifer Carr-Smith, Laurie Coe, Dick Costolo, Hoby Darling, Alex Douzet, Jonathan Edelheit, Wyatt Everhart, Elliott Ferguson, Jennifer Fisher, Bob Fleshner, Rhonda Germany-Ballintyn, Kevin Hart, David Inns, Daniel Johnston, Sarah Kalamchi, Frank Karbe, Michelle Kluz, Emily Kolakowski, Tom Lokar, Dave Long, Ken Lubin, Kristin Machacek Leary, Amy Cozad Magaña, Don Monistere, Tara-Nicholle Nelson, Scott O'Neil, Penny Pritzker, Josh Riff, Larry Senn, Sam Shank, Steven Sinofsky, Jeff Stibel, Robin Thurston, Chris Tsakalakis, Barbara Tulipane, Juan Uro, Rhonda Vetere, Kent Wuthrich, and Strauss Zelnick).

Thank you to all of my colleagues at Heidrick & Struggles who supported this project (including Christina Besozzi Cary, Julia Frenette, Rick Greene, Julian Ha, Jeremy Hanson, Ruben Hillar, Eric Joseph, Jared Oren, Krishnan Rajagopalan, Kendall Sample, Melissa Schmidt, Jason Schmucker, Tom Snyder, Ina Sood, Elmer Velasquez, and Colleen Vogt).

Thank you to all of my friends who provided feedback for this book (including Parker Brill, Alex Chavez, Matt Dershewitz, Lane Brooke Fahy, Jay Kreider, Mark Laurri, Jim Layton, Brian Lee, Nick Macri, Vip Mangal, Paayal Malhotra, Jess Markey, Stu Miller, Laura Neesen, Jim Scott Polsinelli, Rachna Sethi, Stephen Vu, Marc Williams, and Jeremy Zelman).

Thank you to everyone at Gold's Gym, Arlington Sports Conditioning, and Back on My Feet. You all inspire me much more than you know.

Thank you to all the authors and thought leaders who inspire me from afar.

ABOUT THE AUTHOR

Pete Leibman is a leadership consultant, author, and speaker who has been featured on Fox News, CBS Radio, and CNNMoney.com. Earlier in his career, Pete worked as an executive recruiter for Heidrick & Struggles, a leadership advisory firm who serves the majority of the Fortune 500. In his free time, he teaches one of the largest group exercise classes in the Washington, D.C. area, and he has competed in the Obstacle Course Racing (OCR) World Championships. You can meet Pete at WorkStronger.com.

Pete Leibman at work (left) and competing in an obstacle course race (right)

YOU'VE READ *WORK STRONGER*. NOW WHAT?

- **Get your three free bonuses at WorkStronger.com.** These bonuses (a habits assessment, a workbook, and a training series) will help you analyze your current habits and get even better results. You can get these free bonuses at WorkStronger.com.
- **Take *The Stronger Habits Course*:** Would you like more support and guidance in taking your performance to an even higher level? Let Pete guide you step-by-step through his online course on forming stronger habits. You can learn more at https://strongerhabits.com/course.
- **Bring *Work Stronger* into your company:** Would you like to energize your organization and introduce your people to a stronger way of working? Visit https://strongerhabits.com/corporate to learn about content licensing, live workshops, and high performance coaching.

INDEX